C-4983   CAREER EXAMINATION SERIES

This is your
PASSBOOK for...

Transit Customer Service Specialist

Test Preparation Study Guide
Questions & Answers

NLC®

NATIONAL LEARNING CORPORATION®

COPYRIGHT NOTICE

This book is SOLELY intended for, is sold ONLY to, and its use is RESTRICTED to individual, bona fide applicants or candidates who qualify by virtue of having seriously filed applications for appropriate license, certificate, professional and/or promotional advancement, higher school matriculation, scholarship, or other legitimate requirements of education and/or governmental authorities.

This book is NOT intended for use, class instruction, tutoring, training, duplication, copying, reprinting, excerption, or adaptation, etc., by:

1) Other publishers
2) Proprietors and/or Instructors of "Coaching" and/or Preparatory Courses
3) Personnel and/or Training Divisions of commercial, industrial, and governmental organizations
4) Schools, colleges, or universities and/or their departments and staffs, including teachers and other personnel
5) Testing Agencies or Bureaus
6) Study groups which seek by the purchase of a single volume to copy and/or duplicate and/or adapt this material for use by the group as a whole without having purchased individual volumes for each of the members of the group
7) Et al.

Such persons would be in violation of appropriate Federal and State statutes.

PROVISION OF LICENSING AGREEMENTS – Recognized educational, commercial, industrial, and governmental institutions and organizations, and others legitimately engaged in educational pursuits, including training, testing, and measurement activities, may address request for a licensing agreement to the copyright owners, who will determine whether, and under what conditions, including fees and charges, the materials in this book may be used them. In other words, a licensing facility exists for the legitimate use of the material in this book on other than an individual basis. However, it is asseverated and affirmed here that the material in this book CANNOT be used without the receipt of the express permission of such a licensing agreement from the Publishers. Inquiries re licensing should be addressed to the company, attention rights and permissions department.

All rights reserved, including the right of reproduction in whole or in part, in any form or by any means, electronic or mechanical, including photocopying, recording, or by any information storage and retrieval system, without permission in writing from the Publisher.

Copyright © 2024 by
National Learning Corporation

212 Michael Drive, Syosset, NY 11791
(516) 921-8888 • www.passbooks.com
E-mail: info@passbooks.com

PUBLISHED IN THE UNITED STATES OF AMERICA

PASSBOOK® SERIES

THE *PASSBOOK® SERIES* has been created to prepare applicants and candidates for the ultimate academic battlefield – the examination room.

At some time in our lives, each and every one of us may be required to take an examination – for validation, matriculation, admission, qualification, registration, certification, or licensure.

Based on the assumption that every applicant or candidate has met the basic formal educational standards, has taken the required number of courses, and read the necessary texts, the *PASSBOOK® SERIES* furnishes the one special preparation which may assure passing with confidence, instead of failing with insecurity. Examination questions – together with answers – are furnished as the basic vehicle for study so that the mysteries of the examination and its compounding difficulties may be eliminated or diminished by a sure method.

This book is meant to help you pass your examination provided that you qualify and are serious in your objective.

The entire field is reviewed through the huge store of content information which is succinctly presented through a provocative and challenging approach – the question-and-answer method.

A climate of success is established by furnishing the correct answers at the end of each test.

You soon learn to recognize types of questions, forms of questions, and patterns of questioning. You may even begin to anticipate expected outcomes.

You perceive that many questions are repeated or adapted so that you can gain acute insights, which may enable you to score many sure points.

You learn how to confront new questions, or types of questions, and to attack them confidently and work out the correct answers.

You note objectives and emphases, and recognize pitfalls and dangers, so that you may make positive educational adjustments.

Moreover, you are kept fully informed in relation to new concepts, methods, practices, and directions in the field.

You discover that you are actually taking the examination all the time: you are preparing for the examination by "taking" an examination, not by reading extraneous and/or supererogatory textbooks.

In short, this PASSBOOK®, used directedly, should be an important factor in helping you to pass your test.

TRANSIT CUSTOMER SERVICE SPECIALIST

DUTIES
Transit Customer Service Specialists, under close supervision, with limited latitude for independent initiative and judgment, assist and participate in explaining MTA New York City Transit policies and procedures to inquiring customers; receive/record customer complaints, comments and suggestions; dispense information and maps; draft routine replies to customer inquiries; study route schedules of trains and buses to select the most advantageous routes and modes of transportation to reach a destination; provide full and reduced fair media, travel information to callers on special customer inquiry telephone lines; and perform related work.

You will be given a competitive multiple-choice test. A score of at least 70% is required to pass the competitive multiple-choice test.

The competitive multiple-choice test may include questions on the following abilities:

- Written Comprehension: Ability to understand written sentences and paragraphs.
    - Example: *Understanding a training manual's instructions.*
- Written Expression: Ability to use English words or sentences in writing so others will understand.
    - Example: *Typing a customer's complaint into the appropriate database with good grammatical form.*
- Problem Sensitivity: Ability to tell when something is wrong or is likely to go wrong. It includes being able to identify the whole problem as well as the elements of the problem.
    - Example: *Identifying the effect of an employee's recurrent latenesses.*
- Mathematical Reasoning: Ability to understand and organize a problem and then to select a mathematical method or formula to solve the problem. It encompasses reasoning through mathematical problems to determine appropriate operations that can be performed to solve problems. It also includes the understanding or structuring of mathematical problems. The actual manipulation of numbers is not included in this ability.
    - Example: *Determining which mathematical formula to use to calculate the degree to which an employee's call performance has improved month-to-month.*
- Number Facility: Involves the degree to which adding, subtracting, multiplying, and dividing can be done quickly and correctly. These can be steps in other operations such as finding percentages.
    - Example: *Performing a calculation to determine the remaining balance on a MetroCard.*
- Deductive Reasoning: Ability to apply general rules to specific problems to come up with logical answers. It involves deciding if an answer make sense.
    - Example: *Understanding and applying NYCT rules.*
- Inductive Reasoning: Ability to combine separate pieces of information, or specific answers to problems, to form general rules or conclusions.
    - Example: *Understanding why customer service is important and forming appropriate conclusions about how to handle a dissatisfied customer.*
- Information Gathering: Ability to follow correctly a rule or set of rules to arrange

things or actions in a certain order. The rule or sets of rules used must be given. The things or actions to be put in order can include numbers, letters, words, pictures, procedures, sentences, and mathematical or logical operations.
  - Example: *Following a step-by-step rule on how to update a weather advisory status line.*
- Spatial Orientation: Ability to tell where you are in relation to the location of some object or to tell where the object is in relation to you.
  - Example: *Reading a map to train an employee on how to provide a customer with travel directions.*
- Planning and Organizing: Establishing a course of action for self and/or others to accomplish a specific goal; planning proper assignment of personnel and appropriate allocation of resources.
  - Example: *Preparing a list of customer complaints in priority order.*
- Delegation: Utilizing subordinates effectively; allocating decision-making and other responsibilities to the appropriate subordinates.
  - Example: *Assigning a new employee their weekly and daily call targets.*
- Management Control: Establishing procedures to monitor and/or regulate processes, tasks, or activities of subordinates and job activities and responsibilities; taking action to monitor the results of delegated assignments or projects.
  - Example: *Conducting quality control test calls to ensure employees are providing excellent customer service.*
- Development of Subordinartes: Developing the skills and competencies of subordinates through training and developmental activities related to current and future jobs.
  - Example: *Training an employee on how to conduct peer training for new hires.*
- Sensitivity: Actions that indicate a consideration for the feelings and needs of others.
  - Example: *Expressing empathy to a customer who reports losing an item on a subway platform.*
- Analysis: Identifying problems, securing relevant information, relating data from different sources and identifying possible causes of problems.
  - Example: *Using a subway map and a timetable to assist a customer with travel directions.*
- Judgment: Developing alternative courses of action and making decisions based on logical assumptions that reflect factual information.
  - Example: *Determining whether a MetroCard refund is appropriate in light of the customer's situation.*

Customer Service Assessment: If you pass the multiple-choice test, you will be scheduled to take the qualifying customer service assessment as vacancies occur. However, based on the projected number of vacancies, it is possible that not all candidates who pass the multiple-choice test will be scheduled for the qualifying customer service assessment. A score of 70% is required to pass the qualifying customer service assessment. In the qualifying customer service assessment, you may be required to demonstrate the following abilities:
- Oral Comprehension: Ability to understand spoken English words and sentences.
  - Example: *Understanding customers' questions.*
- Oral Expression: Ability to use English words or sentences in speaking so others

will understand.
    - *Example: Communicating the appropriate information or empathetic response to customers.*
- Customer Service Orientation: Predisposition to provide superior service through responsiveness, courtesy and a genuine desire to satisfy customer needs.
    - *Example: Actively listening to a customer who is recounting an incident on the platform.*
- Cognitive Empathy: Ability to understand and anticipate customers' expectations and subsequently engage in appropriate service delivery behaviors.
    - *Example: Understanding the customer's perspective when they express frustration upon learning that the nearest station with a working elevator is farther than expected.*
- Customer Interaction Strategies: Breadth or scope of appropriate strategies used to deal with varying customer needs and situations.
    - *Examples: De-escalating difficult or irate customers. Assisting a customer who speaks a different language.*

HOW TO TAKE A TEST

I. YOU MUST PASS AN EXAMINATION

A. WHAT EVERY CANDIDATE SHOULD KNOW

Examination applicants often ask us for help in preparing for the written test. What can I study in advance? What kinds of questions will be asked? How will the test be given? How will the papers be graded?

As an applicant for a civil service examination, you may be wondering about some of these things. Our purpose here is to suggest effective methods of advance study and to describe civil service examinations.

Your chances for success on this examination can be increased if you know how to prepare. Those "pre-examination jitters" can be reduced if you know what to expect. You can even experience an adventure in good citizenship if you know why civil service exams are given.

B. WHY ARE CIVIL SERVICE EXAMINATIONS GIVEN?

Civil service examinations are important to you in two ways. As a citizen, you want public jobs filled by employees who know how to do their work. As a job seeker, you want a fair chance to compete for that job on an equal footing with other candidates. The best-known means of accomplishing this two-fold goal is the competitive examination.

Exams are widely publicized throughout the nation. They may be administered for jobs in federal, state, city, municipal, town or village governments or agencies.

Any citizen may apply, with some limitations, such as the age or residence of applicants. Your experience and education may be reviewed to see whether you meet the requirements for the particular examination. When these requirements exist, they are reasonable and applied consistently to all applicants. Thus, a competitive examination may cause you some uneasiness now, but it is your privilege and safeguard.

C. HOW ARE CIVIL SERVICE EXAMS DEVELOPED?

Examinations are carefully written by trained technicians who are specialists in the field known as "psychological measurement," in consultation with recognized authorities in the field of work that the test will cover. These experts recommend the subject matter areas or skills to be tested; only those knowledges or skills important to your success on the job are included. The most reliable books and source materials available are used as references. Together, the experts and technicians judge the difficulty level of the questions.

Test technicians know how to phrase questions so that the problem is clearly stated. Their ethics do not permit "trick" or "catch" questions. Questions may have been tried out on sample groups, or subjected to statistical analysis, to determine their usefulness.

Written tests are often used in combination with performance tests, ratings of training and experience, and oral interviews. All of these measures combine to form the best-known means of finding the right person for the right job.

II. HOW TO PASS THE WRITTEN TEST

A. NATURE OF THE EXAMINATION

To prepare intelligently for civil service examinations, you should know how they differ from school examinations you have taken. In school you were assigned certain definite pages to read or subjects to cover. The examination questions were quite detailed and usually emphasized memory. Civil service exams, on the other hand, try to discover your present ability to perform the duties of a position, plus your potentiality to learn these duties. In other words, a civil service exam attempts to predict how successful you will be. Questions cover such a broad area that they cannot be as minute and detailed as school exam questions.

In the public service similar kinds of work, or positions, are grouped together in one "class." This process is known as *position-classification*. All the positions in a class are paid according to the salary range for that class. One class title covers all of these positions, and they are all tested by the same examination.

B. FOUR BASIC STEPS

1) Study the announcement

How, then, can you know what subjects to study? Our best answer is: "Learn as much as possible about the class of positions for which you've applied." The exam will test the knowledge, skills and abilities needed to do the work.

Your most valuable source of information about the position you want is the official exam announcement. This announcement lists the training and experience qualifications. Check these standards and apply only if you come reasonably close to meeting them.

The brief description of the position in the examination announcement offers some clues to the subjects which will be tested. Think about the job itself. Review the duties in your mind. Can you perform them, or are there some in which you are rusty? Fill in the blank spots in your preparation.

Many jurisdictions preview the written test in the exam announcement by including a section called "Knowledge and Abilities Required," "Scope of the Examination," or some similar heading. Here you will find out specifically what fields will be tested.

2) Review your own background

Once you learn in general what the position is all about, and what you need to know to do the work, ask yourself which subjects you already know fairly well and which need improvement. You may wonder whether to concentrate on improving your strong areas or on building some background in your fields of weakness. When the announcement has specified "some knowledge" or "considerable knowledge," or has used adjectives like "beginning principles of..." or "advanced ... methods," you can get a clue as to the number and difficulty of questions to be asked in any given field. More questions, and hence broader coverage, would be included for those subjects which are more important in the work. Now weigh your strengths and weaknesses against the job requirements and prepare accordingly.

3) Determine the level of the position

Another way to tell how intensively you should prepare is to understand the level of the job for which you are applying. Is it the entering level? In other words, is this the position in which beginners in a field of work are hired? Or is it an intermediate or advanced level? Sometimes this is indicated by such words as "Junior" or "Senior" in the class title. Other jurisdictions use Roman numerals to designate the level – Clerk I, Clerk II, for example. The word "Supervisor" sometimes appears in the title. If the level is not indicated by the title, check the description of duties. Will you be working under very close supervision, or will you have responsibility for independent decisions in this work?

4) Choose appropriate study materials

Now that you know the subjects to be examined and the relative amount of each subject to be covered, you can choose suitable study materials. For beginning level jobs, or even advanced ones, if you have a pronounced weakness in some aspect of your training, read a modern, standard textbook in that field. Be sure it is up to date and has general coverage. Such books are normally available at your library, and the librarian will be glad to help you locate one. For entry-level positions, questions of appropriate difficulty are chosen – neither highly advanced questions, nor those too simple. Such questions require careful thought but not advanced training.

If the position for which you are applying is technical or advanced, you will read more advanced, specialized material. If you are already familiar with the basic principles of your field, elementary textbooks would waste your time. Concentrate on advanced textbooks and technical periodicals. Think through the concepts and review difficult problems in your field.

These are all general sources. You can get more ideas on your own initiative, following these leads. For example, training manuals and publications of the government agency which employs workers in your field can be useful, particularly for technical and professional positions. A letter or visit to the government department involved may result in more specific study suggestions, and certainly will provide you with a more definite idea of the exact nature of the position you are seeking.

III. KINDS OF TESTS

Tests are used for purposes other than measuring knowledge and ability to perform specified duties. For some positions, it is equally important to test ability to make adjustments to new situations or to profit from training. In others, basic mental abilities not dependent on information are essential. Questions which test these things may not appear as pertinent to the duties of the position as those which test for knowledge and information. Yet they are often highly important parts of a fair examination. For very general questions, it is almost impossible to help you direct your study efforts. What we can do is to point out some of the more common of these general abilities needed in public service positions and describe some typical questions.

1) General information

Broad, general information has been found useful for predicting job success in some kinds of work. This is tested in a variety of ways, from vocabulary lists to questions about current events. Basic background in some field of work, such as sociology or economics, may be sampled in a group of questions. Often these are principles which have become familiar to most persons through exposure rather than through formal training. It is difficult to advise you how to study for these questions; being alert to the world around you is our best suggestion.

2) Verbal ability

An example of an ability needed in many positions is verbal or language ability. Verbal ability is, in brief, the ability to use and understand words. Vocabulary and grammar tests are typical measures of this ability. Reading comprehension or paragraph interpretation questions are common in many kinds of civil service tests. You are given a paragraph of written material and asked to find its central meaning.

3) Numerical ability
   Number skills can be tested by the familiar arithmetic problem, by checking paired lists of numbers to see which are alike and which are different, or by interpreting charts and graphs. In the latter test, a graph may be printed in the test booklet which you are asked to use as the basis for answering questions.

4) Observation
   A popular test for law-enforcement positions is the observation test. A picture is shown to you for several minutes, then taken away. Questions about the picture test your ability to observe both details and larger elements.

5) Following directions
   In many positions in the public service, the employee must be able to carry out written instructions dependably and accurately. You may be given a chart with several columns, each column listing a variety of information. The questions require you to carry out directions involving the information given in the chart.

6) Skills and aptitudes
   Performance tests effectively measure some manual skills and aptitudes. When the skill is one in which you are trained, such as typing or shorthand, you can practice. These tests are often very much like those given in business school or high school courses. For many of the other skills and aptitudes, however, no short-time preparation can be made. Skills and abilities natural to you or that you have developed throughout your lifetime are being tested.

   Many of the general questions just described provide all the data needed to answer the questions and ask you to use your reasoning ability to find the answers. Your best preparation for these tests, as well as for tests of facts and ideas, is to be at your physical and mental best. You, no doubt, have your own methods of getting into an exam-taking mood and keeping "in shape." The next section lists some ideas on this subject.

IV. KINDS OF QUESTIONS

Only rarely is the "essay" question, which you answer in narrative form, used in civil service tests. Civil service tests are usually of the short-answer type. Full instructions for answering these questions will be given to you at the examination. But in case this is your first experience with short-answer questions and separate answer sheets, here is what you need to know:

1) Multiple-choice Questions
   Most popular of the short-answer questions is the "multiple choice" or "best answer" question. It can be used, for example, to test for factual knowledge, ability to solve problems or judgment in meeting situations found at work.
   A multiple-choice question is normally one of three types—
   - It can begin with an incomplete statement followed by several possible endings. You are to find the one ending which *best* completes the statement, although some of the others may not be entirely wrong.
   - It can also be a complete statement in the form of a question which is answered by choosing one of the statements listed.

- It can be in the form of a problem – again you select the best answer.

Here is an example of a multiple-choice question with a discussion which should give you some clues as to the method for choosing the right answer:

When an employee has a complaint about his assignment, the action which will *best* help him overcome his difficulty is to
    A. discuss his difficulty with his coworkers
    B. take the problem to the head of the organization
    C. take the problem to the person who gave him the assignment
    D. say nothing to anyone about his complaint

In answering this question, you should study each of the choices to find which is best. Consider choice "A" – Certainly an employee may discuss his complaint with fellow employees, but no change or improvement can result, and the complaint remains unresolved. Choice "B" is a poor choice since the head of the organization probably does not know what assignment you have been given, and taking your problem to him is known as "going over the head" of the supervisor. The supervisor, or person who made the assignment, is the person who can clarify it or correct any injustice. Choice "C" is, therefore, correct. To say nothing, as in choice "D," is unwise. Supervisors have and interest in knowing the problems employees are facing, and the employee is seeking a solution to his problem.

2) True/False Questions

The "true/false" or "right/wrong" form of question is sometimes used. Here a complete statement is given. Your job is to decide whether the statement is right or wrong.

SAMPLE: A roaming cell-phone call to a nearby city costs less than a non-roaming call to a distant city.

This statement is wrong, or false, since roaming calls are more expensive.

This is not a complete list of all possible question forms, although most of the others are variations of these common types. You will always get complete directions for answering questions. Be sure you understand *how* to mark your answers – ask questions until you do.

V. RECORDING YOUR ANSWERS

Computer terminals are used more and more today for many different kinds of exams.
For an examination with very few applicants, you may be told to record your answers in the test booklet itself. Separate answer sheets are much more common. If this separate answer sheet is to be scored by machine – and this is often the case – it is highly important that you mark your answers correctly in order to get credit.

An electronic scoring machine is often used in civil service offices because of the speed with which papers can be scored. Machine-scored answer sheets must be marked with a pencil, which will be given to you. This pencil has a high graphite content which responds to the electronic scoring machine. As a matter of fact, stray dots may register as answers, so do not let your pencil rest on the answer sheet while you are pondering the correct answer. Also, if your pencil lead breaks or is otherwise defective, ask for another.

Since the answer sheet will be dropped in a slot in the scoring machine, be careful not to bend the corners or get the paper crumpled.

The answer sheet normally has five vertical columns of numbers, with 30 numbers to a column. These numbers correspond to the question numbers in your test booklet. After each number, going across the page are four or five pairs of dotted lines. These short dotted lines have small letters or numbers above them. The first two pairs may also have a "T" or "F" above the letters. This indicates that the first two pairs only are to be used if the questions are of the true-false type. If the questions are multiple choice, disregard the "T" and "F" and pay attention only to the small letters or numbers.

Answer your questions in the manner of the sample that follows:

32. The largest city in the United States is
    A. Washington, D.C.
    B. New York City
    C. Chicago
    D. Detroit
    E. San Francisco

1) Choose the answer you think is best. (New York City is the largest, so "B" is correct.)
2) Find the row of dotted lines numbered the same as the question you are answering. (Find row number 32)
3) Find the pair of dotted lines corresponding to the answer. (Find the pair of lines under the mark "B.")
4) Make a solid black mark between the dotted lines.

VI. BEFORE THE TEST

Common sense will help you find procedures to follow to get ready for an examination. Too many of us, however, overlook these sensible measures. Indeed, nervousness and fatigue have been found to be the most serious reasons why applicants fail to do their best on civil service tests. Here is a list of reminders:

- Begin your preparation early – Don't wait until the last minute to go scurrying around for books and materials or to find out what the position is all about.
- Prepare continuously – An hour a night for a week is better than an all-night cram session. This has been definitely established. What is more, a night a week for a month will return better dividends than crowding your study into a shorter period of time.
- Locate the place of the exam – You have been sent a notice telling you when and where to report for the examination. If the location is in a different town or otherwise unfamiliar to you, it would be well to inquire the best route and learn something about the building.
- Relax the night before the test – Allow your mind to rest. Do not study at all that night. Plan some mild recreation or diversion; then go to bed early and get a good night's sleep.
- Get up early enough to make a leisurely trip to the place for the test – This way unforeseen events, traffic snarls, unfamiliar buildings, etc. will not upset you.
- Dress comfortably – A written test is not a fashion show. You will be known by number and not by name, so wear something comfortable.

- Leave excess paraphernalia at home – Shopping bags and odd bundles will get in your way. You need bring only the items mentioned in the official notice you received; usually everything you need is provided. Do not bring reference books to the exam. They will only confuse those last minutes and be taken away from you when in the test room.
- Arrive somewhat ahead of time – If because of transportation schedules you must get there very early, bring a newspaper or magazine to take your mind off yourself while waiting.
- Locate the examination room – When you have found the proper room, you will be directed to the seat or part of the room where you will sit. Sometimes you are given a sheet of instructions to read while you are waiting. Do not fill out any forms until you are told to do so; just read them and be prepared.
- Relax and prepare to listen to the instructions
- If you have any physical problem that may keep you from doing your best, be sure to tell the test administrator. If you are sick or in poor health, you really cannot do your best on the exam. You can come back and take the test some other time.

VII. AT THE TEST

The day of the test is here and you have the test booklet in your hand. The temptation to get going is very strong. Caution! There is more to success than knowing the right answers. You must know how to identify your papers and understand variations in the type of short-answer question used in this particular examination. Follow these suggestions for maximum results from your efforts:

1) Cooperate with the monitor

The test administrator has a duty to create a situation in which you can be as much at ease as possible. He will give instructions, tell you when to begin, check to see that you are marking your answer sheet correctly, and so on. He is not there to guard you, although he will see that your competitors do not take unfair advantage. He wants to help you do your best.

2) Listen to all instructions

Don't jump the gun! Wait until you understand all directions. In most civil service tests you get more time than you need to answer the questions. So don't be in a hurry. Read each word of instructions until you clearly understand the meaning. Study the examples, listen to all announcements and follow directions. Ask questions if you do not understand what to do.

3) Identify your papers

Civil service exams are usually identified by number only. You will be assigned a number; you must not put your name on your test papers. Be sure to copy your number correctly. Since more than one exam may be given, copy your exact examination title.

4) Plan your time

Unless you are told that a test is a "speed" or "rate of work" test, speed itself is usually not important. Time enough to answer all the questions will be provided, but this does not mean that you have all day. An overall time limit has been set. Divide the total time (in minutes) by the number of questions to determine the approximate time you have for each question.

5) Do not linger over difficult questions

If you come across a difficult question, mark it with a paper clip (useful to have along) and come back to it when you have been through the booklet. One caution if you do this – be sure to skip a number on your answer sheet as well. Check often to be sure that you have not lost your place and that you are marking in the row numbered the same as the question you are answering.

6) Read the questions

Be sure you know what the question asks! Many capable people are unsuccessful because they failed to *read* the questions correctly.

7) Answer all questions

Unless you have been instructed that a penalty will be deducted for incorrect answers, it is better to guess than to omit a question.

8) Speed tests

It is often better NOT to guess on speed tests. It has been found that on timed tests people are tempted to spend the last few seconds before time is called in marking answers at random – without even reading them – in the hope of picking up a few extra points. To discourage this practice, the instructions may warn you that your score will be "corrected" for guessing. That is, a penalty will be applied. The incorrect answers will be deducted from the correct ones, or some other penalty formula will be used.

9) Review your answers

If you finish before time is called, go back to the questions you guessed or omitted to give them further thought. Review other answers if you have time.

10) Return your test materials

If you are ready to leave before others have finished or time is called, take ALL your materials to the monitor and leave quietly. Never take any test material with you. The monitor can discover whose papers are not complete, and taking a test booklet may be grounds for disqualification.

VIII. EXAMINATION TECHNIQUES

1) Read the general instructions carefully. These are usually printed on the first page of the exam booklet. As a rule, these instructions refer to the timing of the examination; the fact that you should not start work until the signal and must stop work at a signal, etc. If there are any *special* instructions, such as a choice of questions to be answered, make sure that you note this instruction carefully.

2) When you are ready to start work on the examination, that is as soon as the signal has been given, read the instructions to each question booklet, underline any key words or phrases, such as *least, best, outline, describe* and the like. In this way you will tend to answer as requested rather than discover on reviewing your paper that you *listed without describing*, that you selected the *worst* choice rather than the *best* choice, etc.

3) If the examination is of the objective or multiple-choice type – that is, each question will also give a series of possible answers: A, B, C or D, and you are called upon to select the best answer and write the letter next to that answer on your answer paper – it is advisable to start answering each question in turn. There may be anywhere from 50 to 100 such questions in the three or four hours allotted and you can see how much time would be taken if you read through all the questions before beginning to answer any. Furthermore, if you come across a question or group of questions which you know would be difficult to answer, it would undoubtedly affect your handling of all the other questions.

4) If the examination is of the essay type and contains but a few questions, it is a moot point as to whether you should read all the questions before starting to answer any one. Of course, if you are given a choice – say five out of seven and the like – then it is essential to read all the questions so you can eliminate the two that are most difficult. If, however, you are asked to answer all the questions, there may be danger in trying to answer the easiest one first because you may find that you will spend too much time on it. The best technique is to answer the first question, then proceed to the second, etc.

5) Time your answers. Before the exam begins, write down the time it started, then add the time allowed for the examination and write down the time it must be completed, then divide the time available somewhat as follows:
   - If 3-1/2 hours are allowed, that would be 210 minutes. If you have 80 objective-type questions, that would be an average of 2-1/2 minutes per question. Allow yourself no more than 2 minutes per question, or a total of 160 minutes, which will permit about 50 minutes to review.
   - If for the time allotment of 210 minutes there are 7 essay questions to answer, that would average about 30 minutes a question. Give yourself only 25 minutes per question so that you have about 35 minutes to review.

6) The most important instruction is to *read each question* and make sure you know what is wanted. The second most important instruction is to *time yourself properly* so that you answer every question. The third most important instruction is to *answer every question*. Guess if you have to but include something for each question. Remember that you will receive no credit for a blank and will probably receive some credit if you write something in answer to an essay question. If you guess a letter – say "B" for a multiple-choice question – you may have guessed right. If you leave a blank as an answer to a multiple-choice question, the examiners may respect your feelings but it will not add a point to your score. Some exams may penalize you for wrong answers, so in such cases *only*, you may not want to guess unless you have some basis for your answer.

7) Suggestions
   a. Objective-type questions
      1. Examine the question booklet for proper sequence of pages and questions
      2. Read all instructions carefully
      3. Skip any question which seems too difficult; return to it after all other questions have been answered
      4. Apportion your time properly; do not spend too much time on any single question or group of questions

5. Note and underline key words – *all, most, fewest, least, best, worst, same, opposite*, etc.
6. Pay particular attention to negatives
7. Note unusual option, e.g., unduly long, short, complex, different or similar in content to the body of the question
8. Observe the use of "hedging" words – *probably, may, most likely*, etc.
9. Make sure that your answer is put next to the same number as the question
10. Do not second-guess unless you have good reason to believe the second answer is definitely more correct
11. Cross out original answer if you decide another answer is more accurate; do not erase until you are ready to hand your paper in
12. Answer all questions; guess unless instructed otherwise
13. Leave time for review

  b. Essay questions
1. Read each question carefully
2. Determine exactly what is wanted. Underline key words or phrases.
3. Decide on outline or paragraph answer
4. Include many different points and elements unless asked to develop any one or two points or elements
5. Show impartiality by giving pros and cons unless directed to select one side only
6. Make and write down any assumptions you find necessary to answer the questions
7. Watch your English, grammar, punctuation and choice of words
8. Time your answers; don't crowd material

8) Answering the essay question

Most essay questions can be answered by framing the specific response around several key words or ideas. Here are a few such key words or ideas:

M's: manpower, materials, methods, money, management
P's: purpose, program, policy, plan, procedure, practice, problems, pitfalls, personnel, public relations

  a. Six basic steps in handling problems:
1. Preliminary plan and background development
2. Collect information, data and facts
3. Analyze and interpret information, data and facts
4. Analyze and develop solutions as well as make recommendations
5. Prepare report and sell recommendations
6. Install recommendations and follow up effectiveness

  b. Pitfalls to avoid
1. *Taking things for granted* – A statement of the situation does not necessarily imply that each of the elements is necessarily true; for example, a complaint may be invalid and biased so that all that can be taken for granted is that a complaint has been registered

2. *Considering only one side of a situation* – Wherever possible, indicate several alternatives and then point out the reasons you selected the best one
3. *Failing to indicate follow up* – Whenever your answer indicates action on your part, make certain that you will take proper follow-up action to see how successful your recommendations, procedures or actions turn out to be
4. *Taking too long in answering any single question* – Remember to time your answers properly

IX. AFTER THE TEST

Scoring procedures differ in detail among civil service jurisdictions although the general principles are the same. Whether the papers are hand-scored or graded by machine we have described, they are nearly always graded by number. That is, the person who marks the paper knows only the number – never the name – of the applicant. Not until all the papers have been graded will they be matched with names. If other tests, such as training and experience or oral interview ratings have been given, scores will be combined. Different parts of the examination usually have different weights. For example, the written test might count 60 percent of the final grade, and a rating of training and experience 40 percent. In many jurisdictions, veterans will have a certain number of points added to their grades.

After the final grade has been determined, the names are placed in grade order and an eligible list is established. There are various methods for resolving ties between those who get the same final grade – probably the most common is to place first the name of the person whose application was received first. Job offers are made from the eligible list in the order the names appear on it. You will be notified of your grade and your rank as soon as all these computations have been made. This will be done as rapidly as possible.

People who are found to meet the requirements in the announcement are called "eligibles." Their names are put on a list of eligible candidates. An eligible's chances of getting a job depend on how high he stands on this list and how fast agencies are filling jobs from the list.

When a job is to be filled from a list of eligibles, the agency asks for the names of people on the list of eligibles for that job. When the civil service commission receives this request, it sends to the agency the names of the three people highest on this list. Or, if the job to be filled has specialized requirements, the office sends the agency the names of the top three persons who meet these requirements from the general list.

The appointing officer makes a choice from among the three people whose names were sent to him. If the selected person accepts the appointment, the names of the others are put back on the list to be considered for future openings.

That is the rule in hiring from all kinds of eligible lists, whether they are for typist, carpenter, chemist, or something else. For every vacancy, the appointing officer has his choice of any one of the top three eligibles on the list. This explains why the person whose name is on top of the list sometimes does not get an appointment when some of the persons lower on the list do. If the appointing officer chooses the second or third eligible, the No. 1 eligible does not get a job at once, but stays on the list until he is appointed or the list is terminated.

X. HOW TO PASS THE INTERVIEW TEST

The examination for which you applied requires an oral interview test. You have already taken the written test and you are now being called for the interview test – the final part of the formal examination.

You may think that it is not possible to prepare for an interview test and that there are no procedures to follow during an interview. Our purpose is to point out some things you can do in advance that will help you and some good rules to follow and pitfalls to avoid while you are being interviewed.

What is an interview supposed to test?

The written examination is designed to test the technical knowledge and competence of the candidate; the oral is designed to evaluate intangible qualities, not readily measured otherwise, and to establish a list showing the relative fitness of each candidate – as measured against his competitors – for the position sought. Scoring is not on the basis of "right" and "wrong," but on a sliding scale of values ranging from "not passable" to "outstanding." As a matter of fact, it is possible to achieve a relatively low score without a single "incorrect" answer because of evident weakness in the qualities being measured.

Occasionally, an examination may consist entirely of an oral test – either an individual or a group oral. In such cases, information is sought concerning the technical knowledges and abilities of the candidate, since there has been no written examination for this purpose. More commonly, however, an oral test is used to supplement a written examination.

Who conducts interviews?

The composition of oral boards varies among different jurisdictions. In nearly all, a representative of the personnel department serves as chairman. One of the members of the board may be a representative of the department in which the candidate would work. In some cases, "outside experts" are used, and, frequently, a businessman or some other representative of the general public is asked to serve. Labor and management or other special groups may be represented. The aim is to secure the services of experts in the appropriate field.

However the board is composed, it is a good idea (and not at all improper or unethical) to ascertain in advance of the interview who the members are and what groups they represent. When you are introduced to them, you will have some idea of their backgrounds and interests, and at least you will not stutter and stammer over their names.

What should be done before the interview?

While knowledge about the board members is useful and takes some of the surprise element out of the interview, there is other preparation which is more substantive. It *is* possible to prepare for an oral interview – in several ways:

1) Keep a copy of your application and review it carefully before the interview

This may be the only document before the oral board, and the starting point of the interview. Know what education and experience you have listed there, and the sequence and dates of all of it. Sometimes the board will ask you to review the highlights of your experience for them; you should not have to hem and haw doing it.

2) Study the class specification and the examination announcement

Usually, the oral board has one or both of these to guide them. The qualities, characteristics or knowledges required by the position sought are stated in these documents. They offer valuable clues as to the nature of the oral interview. For example, if the job involves supervisory responsibilities, the announcement will usually indicate that knowledge of modern supervisory methods and the qualifications of the candidate as a supervisor will be tested. If so, you can expect such questions, frequently in the form of a hypothetical situation which you are expected to solve. NEVER go into an oral without knowledge of the duties and responsibilities of the job you seek.

3) Think through each qualification required

Try to visualize the kind of questions you would ask if you were a board member. How well could you answer them? Try especially to appraise your own knowledge and background in each area, *measured against the job sought*, and identify any areas in which you are weak. Be critical and realistic – do not flatter yourself.

4) Do some general reading in areas in which you feel you may be weak

For example, if the job involves supervision and your past experience has NOT, some general reading in supervisory methods and practices, particularly in the field of human relations, might be useful. Do NOT study agency procedures or detailed manuals. The oral board will be testing your understanding and capacity, not your memory.

5) Get a good night's sleep and watch your general health and mental attitude

You will want a clear head at the interview. Take care of a cold or any other minor ailment, and of course, no hangovers.

What should be done on the day of the interview?

Now comes the day of the interview itself. Give yourself plenty of time to get there. Plan to arrive somewhat ahead of the scheduled time, particularly if your appointment is in the fore part of the day. If a previous candidate fails to appear, the board might be ready for you a bit early. By early afternoon an oral board is almost invariably behind schedule if there are many candidates, and you may have to wait. Take along a book or magazine to read, or your application to review, but leave any extraneous material in the waiting room when you go in for your interview. In any event, relax and compose yourself.

The matter of dress is important. The board is forming impressions about you – from your experience, your manners, your attitude, and your appearance. Give your personal appearance careful attention. Dress your best, but not your flashiest. Choose conservative, appropriate clothing, and be sure it is immaculate. This is a business interview, and your appearance should indicate that you regard it as such. Besides, being well groomed and properly dressed will help boost your confidence.

Sooner or later, someone will call your name and escort you into the interview room. *This is it.* From here on you are on your own. It is too late for any more preparation. But remember, you asked for this opportunity to prove your fitness, and you are here because your request was granted.

What happens when you go in?

The usual sequence of events will be as follows: The clerk (who is often the board stenographer) will introduce you to the chairman of the oral board, who will introduce you to the other members of the board. Acknowledge the introductions before you sit down. Do not be surprised if you find a microphone facing you or a stenotypist sitting by. Oral interviews are usually recorded in the event of an appeal or other review.

Usually the chairman of the board will open the interview by reviewing the highlights of your education and work experience from your application – primarily for the benefit of the other members of the board, as well as to get the material into the record. Do not interrupt or comment unless there is an error or significant misinterpretation; if that is the case, do not hesitate. But do not quibble about insignificant matters. Also, he will usually ask you some question about your education, experience or your present job – partly to get you to start talking and to establish the interviewing "rapport." He may start the actual questioning, or turn it over to one of the other members. Frequently, each member undertakes the questioning on a particular area, one in which he is perhaps most competent, so you can expect each member to participate in the examination. Because time is limited, you may also expect some rather abrupt switches in the direction the questioning takes, so do not be upset by it. Normally, a board member will not pursue a single line of questioning unless he discovers a particular strength or weakness.

After each member has participated, the chairman will usually ask whether any member has any further questions, then will ask you if you have anything you wish to add. Unless you are expecting this question, it may floor you. Worse, it may start you off on an extended, extemporaneous speech. The board is not usually seeking more information. The question is principally to offer you a last opportunity to present further qualifications or to indicate that you have nothing to add. So, if you feel that a significant qualification or characteristic has been overlooked, it is proper to point it out in a sentence or so. Do not compliment the board on the thoroughness of their examination – they have been sketchy, and you know it. If you wish, merely say, "No thank you, I have nothing further to add." This is a point where you can "talk yourself out" of a good impression or fail to present an important bit of information. Remember, *you close the interview yourself.*

The chairman will then say, "That is all, Mr. _____, thank you." Do not be startled; the interview is over, and quicker than you think. Thank him, gather your belongings and take your leave. Save your sigh of relief for the other side of the door.

How to put your best foot forward

Throughout this entire process, you may feel that the board individually and collectively is trying to pierce your defenses, seek out your hidden weaknesses and embarrass and confuse you. Actually, this is not true. They are obliged to make an appraisal of your qualifications for the job you are seeking, and they want to see you in your best light. Remember, they must interview all candidates and a non-cooperative candidate may become a failure in spite of their best efforts to bring out his qualifications. Here are 15 suggestions that will help you:

1) Be natural – Keep your attitude confident, not cocky

If you are not confident that you can do the job, do not expect the board to be. Do not apologize for your weaknesses, try to bring out your strong points. The board is interested in a positive, not negative, presentation. Cockiness will antagonize any board member and make him wonder if you are covering up a weakness by a false show of strength.

2) Get comfortable, but don't lounge or sprawl

Sit erectly but not stiffly. A careless posture may lead the board to conclude that you are careless in other things, or at least that you are not impressed by the importance of the occasion. Either conclusion is natural, even if incorrect. Do not fuss with your clothing, a pencil or an ashtray. Your hands may occasionally be useful to emphasize a point; do not let them become a point of distraction.

3) Do not wisecrack or make small talk

This is a serious situation, and your attitude should show that you consider it as such. Further, the time of the board is limited – they do not want to waste it, and neither should you.

4) Do not exaggerate your experience or abilities

In the first place, from information in the application or other interviews and sources, the board may know more about you than you think. Secondly, you probably will not get away with it. An experienced board is rather adept at spotting such a situation, so do not take the chance.

5) If you know a board member, do not make a point of it, yet do not hide it

Certainly you are not fooling him, and probably not the other members of the board. Do not try to take advantage of your acquaintanceship – it will probably do you little good.

6) Do not dominate the interview

Let the board do that. They will give you the clues – do not assume that you have to do all the talking. Realize that the board has a number of questions to ask you, and do not try to take up all the interview time by showing off your extensive knowledge of the answer to the first one.

7) Be attentive

You only have 20 minutes or so, and you should keep your attention at its sharpest throughout. When a member is addressing a problem or question to you, give him your undivided attention. Address your reply principally to him, but do not exclude the other board members.

8) Do not interrupt

A board member may be stating a problem for you to analyze. He will ask you a question when the time comes. Let him state the problem, and wait for the question.

9) Make sure you understand the question

Do not try to answer until you are sure what the question is. If it is not clear, restate it in your own words or ask the board member to clarify it for you. However, do not haggle about minor elements.

10) Reply promptly but not hastily

A common entry on oral board rating sheets is "candidate responded readily," or "candidate hesitated in replies." Respond as promptly and quickly as you can, but do not jump to a hasty, ill-considered answer.

11) Do not be peremptory in your answers

A brief answer is proper – but do not fire your answer back. That is a losing game from your point of view. The board member can probably ask questions much faster than you can answer them.

12) Do not try to create the answer you think the board member wants

He is interested in what kind of mind you have and how it works – not in playing games. Furthermore, he can usually spot this practice and will actually grade you down on it.

13) Do not switch sides in your reply merely to agree with a board member

Frequently, a member will take a contrary position merely to draw you out and to see if you are willing and able to defend your point of view. Do not start a debate, yet do not surrender a good position. If a position is worth taking, it is worth defending.

14) Do not be afraid to admit an error in judgment if you are shown to be wrong

The board knows that you are forced to reply without any opportunity for careful consideration. Your answer may be demonstrably wrong. If so, admit it and get on with the interview.

15) Do not dwell at length on your present job

The opening question may relate to your present assignment. Answer the question but do not go into an extended discussion. You are being examined for a *new* job, not your present one. As a matter of fact, try to phrase ALL your answers in terms of the job for which you are being examined.

Basis of Rating

Probably you will forget most of these "do's" and "don'ts" when you walk into the oral interview room. Even remembering them all will not ensure you a passing grade. Perhaps you did not have the qualifications in the first place. But remembering them will help you to put your best foot forward, without treading on the toes of the board members.

Rumor and popular opinion to the contrary notwithstanding, an oral board wants you to make the best appearance possible. They know you are under pressure – but they also want to see how you respond to it as a guide to what your reaction would be under the pressures of the job you seek. They will be influenced by the degree of poise you display, the personal traits you show and the manner in which you respond.

ABOUT THIS BOOK

This book contains tests divided into Examination Sections. Go through each test, answering every question in the margin. We have also attached a sample answer sheet at the back of the book that can be removed and used. At the end of each test look at the answer key and check your answers. On the ones you got wrong, look at the right answer choice and learn. Do not fill in the answers first. Do not memorize the questions and answers, but understand the answer and principles involved. On your test, the questions will likely be different from the samples. Questions are changed and new ones added. If you understand these past questions you should have success with any changes that arise. Tests may consist of several types of questions. We have additional books on each subject should more study be advisable or necessary for you. Finally, the more you study, the better prepared you will be. This book is intended to be the last thing you study before you walk into the examination room. Prior study of relevant texts is also recommended. NLC publishes some of these in our Fundamental Series. Knowledge and good sense are important factors in passing your exam. Good luck also helps. So now study this Passbook, absorb the material contained within and take that knowledge into the examination. Then do your best to pass that exam.

EXAMINATION SECTION

EXAMINATION SECTION
TEST 1

DIRECTIONS: Each question or incomplete statement is followed by several suggested answers or completions. Select the one that BEST answers the question or completes the statement. *PRINT THE LETTER OF THE CORRECT ANSWER IN THE SPACE AT THE RIGHT.*

1. A woman in her mid-30s comes up to your desk and asks you how she can apply to work at your office. You do not know the immediate answer to that question.
 Which of the following would be the BEST way to respond to her request?
    A. Tell her what sounds like the right answer
    B. Tell her to talk to your boss and show her how to do that
    C. Explain you are not allowed to give out confidential information to the public
    D. Inform her that you do not know right now, but you will find out

    1.____

2. A person approaches the customer service desk and asks you to do something that you are ultimately unable to do.
 Which of the following should you avoid doing next?
    A. Opening your policy handbook and reading from it verbatim
    B. Clarifying why you cannot do what he or she is asking of you
    C. Crafting detailed and precise statements
    D. Giving the person alternative options

    2.____

3. When talking to someone from the public, which of the following statements would be LEAST frustrating for the customer to hear?
    A. "You'll have to..."   B. "Mr. X will be back at any moment..."
    C. "Let me see what I can do..."   D. "I'll do my best..."

    3.____

4. Your office recently received a letter from an individual expressing extreme frustration and disappointment at how it was handling the customer's problems. You have written an apology letter and are reviewing it before sending it to the customer.
 You should ensure the letter is NOT
    A. sincere   B. official
    C. personal   D. sent immediately

    4.____

5. If you are unable to provide a certain service or product with dependability and accuracy, it would be defined as a lack of
    A. courtesy   B. reliability   C. assurance   D. responsiveness

    5.____

1

6. As most civil service employees know, customer feedback can be, and usually is, an integral part of customer service.
   Which of the following feedback scenarios would be MOST useful to your organization?
   A. When it is an ongoing feedback system
   B. When centered on internal customers
   C. When it is focused on only a few indicators
   D. When every employee can see the feedback coming in

7. Which of the following is the LEAST important factor in making sure a customer survey is a valuable tool for your company?
   A. Taking every precaution to ensure the survey input is maintained in a confidential manner
   B. Making sure the customers believe in the confidentiality of the survey
   C. Ensuring confidentiality by having an outside company administer the survey
   D. Making sure the employees buy in and promote the survey to customers

8. Which of the following would NOT be considered part of the resolution process when identifying and dealing with a customers' problems?
   A. Following up with the customer after resolving the issue
   B. Listening and responding to each complaint the customer registers
   C. Giving the customer what they originally requested
   D. Promising the customer whatever you need to

9. A customer approaches you with a complaint. You want to arrive at a fair solution to the problem.
   What is the FIRST step you should take in this situation?
   A. Immediately defend your company from any customer criticisms
   B. Listen to the customer describe their problem
   C. Ask the customer questions to confirm the type of problem they are having
   D. Determine a solution to the customer's problem(s)

10. If you are dealing with a customer in a prompt manner when addressing their complaints or issues, which of the following are you demonstrating?
    A. Assurance   B. Empathy
    C. Responsiveness   D. Reliability

11. Steve has recently been hired to work at the postal office in town. A customer comes into the office to complain about the number of packages of his they have lost over the past year.
    When Steve attempts to help the upset customer, what should he make sure to do FIRST?
    He should
    A. check into how legitimate the customer's complaints are and see if he can do anything about the missing packages
    B. just let the customer blow off some steam and chalk it up to an emotional outburst

C. ask for help from his boss to see how to handle the situation
D. assume the complaints are accurate and immediately attempt to correct them

12. How should a service representative react when a customer first presents them with a request?
    A. Apologize
    B. Greet them in a friendly manner
    C. Read from the employee handbook about the request
    D. Ask the customer to clarify information

13. In order to assuage a customer's frustration, which of the following should a civil service employee demonstrate?
    A. Compassion   B. Indifference   C. Surprise   D. Agreement

14. A customer comes into the office requesting that your organization do something for them that you know is not part of organization policy.
    Your FIRST responsibility would be to
    A. pass the customer on to higher management to deal with the issue
    B. persuade the customer to believe that the organization can grant their request
    C. mold expectations so they more closely resemble what the organization can do for the customer
    D. tell the customer there is no way you can comply with their request

15. Of the following potential distractors, which one MOST prevents a civil service employee from displaying good listening skills while a customer is speaking?
    A. Cell phones or checking e-mail
    B. Asking superfluous questions
    C. Background office noise
    D. Interrupting the customer to speak with colleagues

16. If you are in a situation where you have to deliver a negative response to a customer, it is often better to say _____ instead of just saying "no"?
    A. "I will try to..."   B. "You can..."
    C. "Our policy does not allow..."   D. "I do not believe..."

17. You are working one-on-one with a customer.
    Which of the following would be the MOST appropriate body language to display?
    A. Make frowning faces
    B. Stare at a spot over the customer's shoulder
    C. Lean in toward the customer
    D. Cross your arms while they speak

18. The majority of communication in face-to-face meetings with customers is shown through
    A. word choice   B. tone
    C. clothing choice   D. body language

19. A customer angrily approaches you at your service desk and starts expressing his frustration with recent actions by your department.
    Which of the following should be your FIRST responses to the customer?
    A. Listen to the person, then express understanding and apologize for how they have been negatively affected by your department's action
    B. Interrupt them while they are speaking and tell them to calm down or you will not help them
    C. Give them an explanation of why your department took the actions they did
    D. None of the above

    19.____

20. Of the following services, which one is NOT customized to a specific individual's needs?
    A. Hair salon
    B. Elementary education
    C. Computer counseling
    D. Dental care

    20.____

21. Which of the following civil service employees demonstrates excellent customer service?
    A. A park ranger who minimizes public interaction and contact
    B. The Postal Service employee who sees the customer as a commodity
    C. The office clerk who spends a lot of time with customers sharing personal stories and anecdotes
    D. A DMV employee with open body language and direct communication

    21.____

22. It is important to have excellent knowledge of services and products, if applicable, when interacting with consumers because
    A. you can demonstrate your knowledge and impress the customer
    B. your organization can have a higher margin of profit regardless of customer benefit
    C. the customer's needs can best be matched with appropriate services/products
    D. you can look good to your superiors and keep your job

    22.____

23. A park ranger has recently been coming to a kids' camp dirty and unkempt. Even though her job requires her to be outside at ties, why should she still care about her personal appearance?
    A. To speed up her service to the public
    B. So she is seen as a professional in her field
    C. It would help her organizational skills
    D. To show her level of expertise as a park ranger

    23.____

24. How could guided conversation be a positive with interacting with the public?
    A. It allows you to anticipate a person's needs and expectations.
    B. Most people know what they want even before they show up to your office.
    C. It creates the impression of friendliness.
    D. It helps time move faster.

    24.____

25. In the event a conflict or crisis arises, which of the following would be considered a POOR action to take when interacting with the public?
    A. Provide a constant flow of information
    B. Put the public's needs first
    C. Avoid saying "No Comment" as much as possible
    D. Assign multiple spokespeople so media calls can be dealt with efficiently

KEY (CORRECT ANSWERS)

1.	D	11.	A
2.	A	12.	D
3.	C	13.	A
4.	B	14.	C
5.	B	15.	D
6.	A	16.	B
7.	C	17.	C
8.	D	18.	D
9.	B	19.	A
10.	C	20.	B

21.	D
22.	C
23.	B
24.	A
25.	D

TEST 2

DIRECTIONS: Each question or incomplete statement is followed by several suggested answers or completions. Select the one that BEST answers the question or completes the statement. *PRINT THE LETTER OF THE CORRECT ANSWER IN THE SPACE AT THE RIGHT.*

1. John Smith answers a caller who struggles to understand a convoluted policy of your agency.
   How should he handle the customer's question?
   A. Tell the caller to go to the agency's website
   B. He should be honest and say he does not know the answer to the question
   C. John should explain the policy in general terms and refer them to a written version of the policy
   D. Tell the caller to talk to his supervisor and then give the caller the supervisor's extension

1.____

2. While meeting with a group of young campers at the local parks and recreation office, you conduct a lecture on the importance of avoiding dangerous plants near the forest.
   What can you do to make sure your inexperienced audience remembers the main points of your presentation?
   A. Use flashy visuals that catch the eye
   B. Repeat and emphasize your points
   C. Make jokes so the presentation is livelier
   D. Allow the campers to ask questions at the end of the presentation

2.____

3. A park ranger is about to deliver a speech at a public conservation meeting. Which of the following is the MOST important thing to keep in mind as he preps for the presentation?
   A. How large the audience is
   B. Whether or not he will be able to use visual aids
   C. If he will have time to use charts and graphs
   D. Audience interests

3.____

4. Jerry receives a letter from a customer and is about to shred it without reading. When you stop him, he says that there is no reason to read it because you cannot learn very much from letters you receive from the public.
   Which of the following should you tell him in order to convince him that reading letters sent from the public is beneficial and necessary?
   A. These public letters can give us a feel for how we are meeting customer needs.
   B. Letters from the public tell us how well our informational efforts are working.
   C. These letters can inform us of what additional training we may need.
   D. The letters can tell us whether public information processes need to be changed or not.

4.____

5. Ms. Johnson is a volunteer with the Parks and Recreation Department and her children also attend various summer programs through the district. She comes to you today to complain that one of her children was not allowed to join a program because they missed the sign-up by one day. She calls your staff a bunch of "morons" and complains that your department's actions are creating serious issues for her.
How should you handle this situation?
   A. Let Ms. Johnson rant until she gets it out of her system
   B. Tell her you cannot help her and will ask her to leave if she cannot stop referring to your colleagues as "morons"
   C. Refer Ms. Johnson to your boss
   D. Try to alter the tone of the conversation to a more objective and less emotional discussion of Ms. Johnson's problems

5.____

6. A civil service employee is tasked with moderating a town hall meeting regarding child safety, but he knows that residents will be attending the meeting with different motives.
How can the employee make sure the town hall meeting is as beneficial and informational as possible?
   A. Ask attendees to be open to changing their opinions and preferences
   B. Start out by recognizing the various motives but also stress the common objectives and interests
   C. Call out individuals who you know have specific reasons for attending and put them on the spot
   D. Cancel the meeting and avoid rescheduling it until you can be sure everyone is on the same page

6.____

7. During the question-and-answer session at the end of a presentation, a member of the public makes a suggestion that you deem not only practical but worthy of further discussion.
How should you react to this?
   A. Tell them you will let the appropriate people know of the suggestion
   B. Tell the person you concur with them wholeheartedly
   C. Let the person know you think it is a good idea but you cannot make decisions based on suggestions during Q and A
   D. Even though the suggestion is good, tell the person that someone in your organization has probably already thought of the idea

7.____

8. When in a conversation with a group of local residents, what is the BIGGEST problem with one or two people dominating the conversation?
   A. Your interaction could take longer than it should
   B. Some people will become distracted and not focus on the meeting anymore
   C. The other member of the group may not have an opportunity to share their opinions
   D. None of the above

8.____

9. You receive a phone call at the village hall, but the information being requested would need to come from the police station.
   How should you respond to the caller?
   A. Give them the police station's website and wish them well
   B. Tell them you are not responsible for their request
   C. Refer them to the police station's number and information
   D. Provide them with the information as best as you can

10. Which of the following should almost always be avoided when interacting with a member of the community?
    A. Contentious matters
    B. Topics about financial material
    C. Rules and regulations
    D. Technical lingo or jargon

11. When people use inflammatory language laced with obscenities, a town employee should
    A. refuse to continue the dialogue if the person cannot stop using the offensive language
    B. tell the person to talk to your supervisor
    C. allow the person to finish "venting" before attempting to find a solution to the problem
    D. hang up if on the phone; if in person, leave the area and ask the individual to leave as well

12. A member of the public has sent your agency a letter.
    Which of the following will help you figure out how much explaining you need to do when writing a response?
    A. Go to the agency website and search for how much explanation is provided there
    B. Take out the original customer letter and study it
    C. Presume the person who wrote the letter already has a working knowledge of the subject and thus will not require a lot of background explanation
    D. Look at past letters sent by your agency

13. During an informational meeting with local townspeople, a man makes a suggestion for a new town measure that is based on incorrect information and is impractical.
    What is the BEST way to handle a situation such as this?
    A. Ask if anyone else in attendance would like to respond to the suggestion
    B. Tell the person it is a great idea even though you are aware of its folly
    C. Thank the man for coming and tell everyone you always welcome their suggestions
    D. Inform the person that his/her comment clearly reflects an inferior knowledge about the subject

14. A member from the public calls your office about negative comments he has heard about one of your programs. You believe the comments were made by someone who had inaccurate material, but you are not completely certain of that because you are not directly involved with the program.

What is the BEST way to handle this situation?
- A. Tell the caller you will analyze the situation in depth and then call them back
- B. Tell the caller the evidence on which they have based their judgment is not supported
- C. Explain that your office has a "No Comment" policy regarding negative comments
- D. Let the caller know you are not involved with the program directly, and tell them to call the person who is

15. Which of the following quotes reflects the BEST way to handle an angry resident that keeps interrupting during a village meeting?
    - A. "I am here as a volunteer and I do not need this."
    - B. "I understand your anger, but we have quite a bit of information to cover tonight, so in fairness to everyone else, please let me continue."
    - C. "Every crowd has one black sheep in it."
    - D. "Sir, (or Ma'am) if you cannot stop interjecting, I will have security escort you from the premises."

16. Of the following, which is an example of nonverbal communication?
    - A. Frowning
    - B. Hand signs
    - C. A "21 Gun Salute"
    - D. All of the above

17. Residents of Masterton, Georgia, were recently made aware that the main road into and out of town will be under construction for the next four years. The construction will make travel time much more difficult for the citizens and they have demanded a meeting with your department. You are tasked with creating a presentation to explain to them why the construction is necessary.
    At the start of the presentation, you should
    - A. make a joke to lighten the mood
    - B. state the purpose of your presentation
    - C. provide a detailed account of the history behind the project
    - D. make a call to action

18. When a member of the public asks questions that are confusing or you do not understand right away, what is the BEST way to handle this situation?
    - A. Answer the question as you understand it
    - B. Stick to generalizations dealing with the subject of the question
    - C. Rephrase the question and ask the person if you understood what they were asking
    - D. Ask the person to repeat the question

19. When preparing for a public interaction, which of the following situations would be MOST appropriate to include handouts?
    - A. If you want to help the attendees remember important information after the interaction is over
    - B. If you want to keep the interaction short

C. When you want to remember key points to talk about
D. When you do not want attendees to have to pay attention during the interaction

20. John is in the process of handling a phone call when a local citizen approaches his desk to ask a question. Neither the caller nor the visitor seem to be in a crisis.
What should John do in this scenario?
    A. Keep talking with the caller until he is finished. Then tell the visitor he is sorry for making them wait.
    B. Remain on the phone with the caller but look up at the visitor every once and awhile so they know he has not forgotten about them.
    C. Tell the caller he has a visitor, so the conversation needs to end.
    D. Tell the visitor he will be with them as soon as he finishes the phone call.

20.____

21. When engaged in conversation with another person, which communication technique is MOST likely to ensure you comprehend fully what the other person to trying to communicate to you?
    A. Repeat back to the person what you think they are communicating
    B. Continual eye contact
    C. Making sure the person speaks slowly
    D. Nodding your head while they speak

21.____

22. You encounter someone who is frustrated about a situation and needs to vent by talking it out before they can move onto a productive conversation.
When a situation is like this, it is often BEST to
    A. recommend various strategies for calming down
    B. Ask to be excused from the conversation without offering why
    C. Explain to the person that it is unproductive to behave the way they are currently behaving
    D. Acknowledge that venting is a crucial step to moving past the emotions and allow the person to express his or her feelings

23.____

23. Which of the following is NOT an example of active listening?
    A. Taking notes
    B. Referring the customer to the manager after they are done speaking
    C. Using phrases like "I see" or "Go on"
    D. Repeating back to the customer what you've heard

23.____

24. Which of the following questions would be classified as a clarification question?
    A. "How long have you sold spoiled meat?"
    B. "Do you like our brand?"
    C. "You mentioned you liked this merchandise. How would you feel about this?"
    D. None of the above

24.____

25. When interacting with a member of the public, which of the following words should you avoid using as it is not positive as perceived by most people? 25.____
    A. "Absolutely"
    B. "You are welcome"
    C. "Here's what I can do"
    D. "I'll do my best"

KEY (CORRECT ANSWERS)

1. C
2. B
3. D
4. A
5. D

6. B
7. A
8. C
9. C
10. D

11. A
12. B
13. C
14. A
15. B

16. D
17. B
18. C
19. A
20. D

21. A
22. D
23. B
24. C
25. D

EXAMINATION SECTION

TEST 1

DIRECTIONS: Each question or incomplete statement is followed by several suggested answers or completions. Select the one that BEST answers the question or completes the statement. *PRINT THE LETTER OF THE CORRECT ANSWER IN THE SPACE AT THE RIGHT.*

1. Which of the following is a behavior that can impact customer service?   1._____
   A. Greeting customers promptly
   B. Believing in a positive mission statement
   C. Giving great service
   D. Poor work attitude

2. What are vital behaviors?   2._____
   A. Ones that are mandated by law
   B. Specific actions that have the maximum impact on customer service
   C. Of no particular importance when influencing employees
   D. The same as good attitudes

3. Of the following, the MOST effective icebreaker when greeting a customer would be: 3._____
   A. Talking about local interests such as a sports team or the weather
   B. Expression appreciation for the customer visiting you today
   C. Finding out and expressing interest in something the customer shows interest in
   D. All of the above

4. Which of the following actions would get customers to interact with you and, therefore, the organization you represent?   4._____
   A. Inviting the customers to fill out paperwork
   B. Help the customer sample the company's culture
   C. Both A and B
   D. None of the above

5. Of the following options, the BIGGEST issue with not greeting a customer promptly is: 5._____
   A. The customer might not leave as quickly as you'd like them to
   B. The organization misses an opportunity to establish a positive relationship
   C. They may estimate that their wait was shorter than it actually was
   D. Both A and C

6. Which of the following actions is it important to take when someone makes an oral presentation to a large group of customers?   6._____
   A. Relax the audience by moving back and forth when speaking
   B. Avoid eye contact with anyone in the audience
   C. Speak loudly enough for all to hear your message
   D. Turn your back to the audience when presenting visual aids

7. Of the following techniques for writing effective communication (i.e., business letters) to customers, which of the following helps a person be consistently on message the MOST?
   A. Preparing outlines
   B. Development and inclusion of charts
   C. Consulting references
   D. Asking questions

8. Persuasive messages that ask a person to do something should be communicated in a way that makes it easy for that person to
   A. plan accordingly
   B. answer politely
   C. organize logically
   D. respond positively

9. If an organization wishes to emphasize customer service skills such as courtesy and friendliness, when should said organization focus on these skills?
   A. When designing their facilities
   B. During market research
   C. When meeting for technology planning
   D. During the hiring process

10. If an organization realizes they need to improve their technology to better meet customer demands and desires, this would have to result from a business activity known as
    A. continuity improvement
    B. business process management
    C. employee training and in-service
    D. organizational positioning

11. When in the distribution channel business, what is an important thing to keep in mind concerning customers?
    A. Most expect low service levels.
    B. Many want immediate delivery.
    C. Everyone defines service differently.
    D. A number of customers tend to refuse late shipments.

12. When persuading a customer to go along with a proposed change from their initial query, you should
    A. explain how the change will benefit them
    B. tell them you have a better way of doing things
    C. minimize the amount of information you share with them
    D. reinforce your ideas with facts and statistics

13. Which of the following statements regarding using the internet to administer questionnaires is TRUE?
    A. Interviewers are more likely to influence respondents' answers online.
    B. Online questionnaires require more time for data entry and collection.
    C. Respondents are more likely to misunderstand online questionnaires.
    D. Data entry and administrative costs are higher for online questionnaires.

14. After a series of governmental scandals, a public service organization wants the public to perceive it as more trustworthy and embarks on an advertising campaign to aid the makeover. What goal does this illustrate?
    A. Projecting a certain image
    B. Achieving stability
    C. Increasing customer service and productivity
    D. All of the above

14.____

15. When presenting information to a small group of customers, you decided to use presentation software to prepare your multimedia presentation.
    What is the purpose of using this software?
    A. To develop websites
    B. To maintain customer files
    C. To access online resources
    D. To support your report findings

15.____

16. A current trend in hospitality of customers is to build loyal customer relationships and enhance service levels by optimizing the use of
    A. independent agents
    B. internet web sites
    C. satellite roving devices
    D. service rating advisors

16.____

17. Which of the following would be an excellent example of an employee empathizing with a customer's objection?
    A. "I understand how you feel."
    B. "You must think the price is too high."
    C. "Everyone knows this is how this process works."
    D. "I really don't see what you don't understand about this."

17.____

18. Customer service experts who use the services and products they are in charge of dispensing are able to suggest appropriate substitute services and products because of their own personal
    A. preference
    B. feelings
    C. experience
    D. opinion

18.____

19. An employee should always attempt to answer a customer's questions thoroughly and explain the benefits of the service so that the customer will
    A. make a quicker decision
    B. be in a state of indecision
    C. think about making a decision
    D. feel better about the purchasing decision

19.____

20. One should be able to adjust his customer service style from one customer to another so that he can appeal to each customer's
    A. natural aptitude
    B. unique personality
    C. hidden objection
    D. internal ability

20.____

21. In order to attract customers and encourage them to visit the facilities, what do many organizations do?
    A. Market trips
    B. Trade shows
    C. Press kits
    D. Special events

21.____

22. What kind of question is a person asking if they ask the following: "What level of service would you like today?" 22.____
    A. Interpretive
    B. Impersonal
    C. Open-ended
    D. Assumptive

23. Your organization holds a meeting to identify community issues with which they can involve themselves. 23.____
    Which of the following options should the organization consider when deciding which community issue to involve themselves with?
    It should
    A. contribute to the social good
    B. earn a reasonable profit
    C. boost employee loyalty
    D. support controversial topics

24. If a person's thoughts, emotions, and physical sensations interfere with their listening skills, that is referred to as 24.____
    A. cultural diversity
    B. internal noise
    C. cultural norms
    D. external noise

25. Which of the following is NOT a characteristic of information literacy? 25.____
    The ability to
    A. use information to manipulate others
    B. determine what information is needed for a presentation
    C. find information relevant to a topic
    D. use information to create new knowledge

KEY (CORRECT ANSWERS)

1.	A		11.	C
2.	B		12.	A
3.	D		13.	C
4.	C		14.	A
5.	B		15.	D
6.	C		16.	B
7.	A		17.	A
8.	D		18.	C
9.	D		19.	D
10.	B		20.	B

21. D
22. C
23. A
24. B
25. A

TEST 2

DIRECTIONS: Each question or incomplete statement is followed by several suggested answers or completions. Select the one that BEST answers the question or completes the statement. *PRINT THE LETTER OF THE CORRECT ANSWER IN THE SPACE AT THE RIGHT.*

1. When preparing to deliver a speech, what is the purpose of writing key points on notecards and then placing those cards in order of their importance? 1.____
    A. To verify their authenticity
    B. To access files
    C. To revise facts
    D. To organize information

2. An employee who is originally from Ecuador meets with a client from London, England and when the employee attempts to shake the client's hand, the client backs away. 2.____
   What cultural issue should the employee be aware of next time to avoid this misstep?
    A. Punctuality
    B. Personal space preferences
    C. Appearance
    D. Language variances

3. An employee who demonstrates self-confidence has which of the following characteristics? 3.____
    A. They take few risks because they fear making mistakes.
    B. They exhibit aggressive behavior when expressing their opinion.
    C. They realize that mistakes are a part of personal growth.
    D. They are overly concerned with what others say about them.

4. An employee is working with a client for an hour going over the features of a service they offer when the client interrupts and says, "I can find this service for a lot less than what you are offer. Your price is preposterous!" 4.____
   If the employee wishes to reply in the most professional manner as possible, they would do which of the following?
    A. Attempt to explain the benefits of the service from this organization over another.
    B. Stop helping the client and begin to find someone else to help.
    C. Ask a supervisor to help convince the client to purchase the service there.
    D. Thank the client politely for coming in today.

5. You are working with a customer who asks you questions about aspects of the organization that you are clearly not familiar with. A coworker overhears the conversation and offers to help. 5.____
   What is the FIRST thing you should do?
    A. Politely refuse the help and attempt to answer the customer's questions anyway.
    B. Accept the offer of help and listen to the answers the coworker gives to the customer.
    C. Ignore the coworker. They only want to look good in front of your supervisor.
    D. Let the other associate take over and look for a new customer to help.

6. A customer comes up to an employee with a broken item from the store. They say they bought the item a month ago and now it does not work. What is the FIRST thing the employee should do?
    A. "With this kind of item, it's best you check simple things like the batteries first. I will check for you."
    B. "We've never had anyone return this item before. What did you or your child do to it?"
    C. "Are you sure you bought this item at our store? Do you have your receipt?"
    D. "We've had a lot of issues with that item. You should probably contact the manufacturer."

7. When a person first encounters an employee and forms a lasting mental image of that employee and, therefore, the organization, that is called
    A. attitude impact
    B. self-confidence
    C. first impression
    D. workplace ethics

8. Which of the following convey to clients that a person is professional?
    A. No wrinkles, creases or stains
    B. No large, loud prints
    C. Well-tailored, formal clothing
    D. All of the above

9. An employee is put in charge of email communications for the organization and asks you for help.
   Which of the following would NOT be considered good email etiquette?
    A. Keeping emails brief and to the point
    B. Putting the purpose of the email in the subject field
    C. Sending humorous YouTube videos and personal emails to customers
    D. Using a signature that includes contact information that follows your message

10. An employee is holding a meeting for clients and is just about to conclude when another client shows up late.
    Which of the following actions would be the BEST to take?
    A. Thank the client for stopping by and pause the meeting momentarily to fill the client in on what they missed.
    B. Once the meeting is over, remind the client that punctuality is incredibly important to your organization. Then once they seem to understand the importance of being on time, fill them in on what they missed.
    C. Openly criticize the client in front of everyone else for being tardy. Once you've criticized them, fill them in on what they missed.
    D. Slightly nod to the client when they enter, but continue the meeting without bringing them up to speed. Once the meeting concludes, fill the client in if the wish to be brought up to speed.

11. You are running 15 minutes late to a meeting with a client.　　　　　　　　　　11._____
    What should you do?
    A. Call the client and tell them you will be there in a few minutes.
    B. The client won't mind waiting. Fifteen minutes is not that long of a wait.
    C. Have your coworker talk to the client and tell them you were involved in a minor traffic accident that is causing you to be delayed.
    D. Pretend like you thought the meeting was supposed to be on a different day. Send an email apologizing for the inconvenience.

12. A longtime friend has stopped at your work to visit you before they fly home.　　12._____
    You are currently working with customers when he shows up.
    What should you do?
    A. Have your friend join the meeting and introduce him to your customers.
    B. Tell your friend to wait in the break room/cafeteria and meet him when you finish up your meeting with the customers.
    C. Stop the meeting immediately and tell the customers to reschedule with you tomorrow. You also let them know they will have priority in terms of meeting times.
    D. Speed through the rest of the meeting and do not stop to ask if anyone has any questions. Then find your friend afterwards.

13. A coworker is currently working with customers when you notice your favorite　　13._____
    song starts playing from your computer. You
    A. dance around the office after blasting the music on your speakers
    B. listen to the music with your headphones at a loud volume so that the customers can hear a muted version of the song
    C. listen to the music with your headphones in at a low volume so that you do not disturb others and are still accessible in case coworkers/customers need you
    D. listen to your music with noise-cancelling headphones, so that you cannot hear others if they request your attention

14. You have an important meeting with customers and they will be meeting you　　14._____
    around dinner time.
    Where should you bring them for the dinner meeting?
    A. Ask them their preference for food and pick the corresponding restaurant.
    B. An upscale French restaurant known for its romantic ambience
    C. A sports bar that will be airing an important playoff game
    D. Order Chinese food and invite them to the office

15. An employee has an important presentation in front of customers today, but it　　15._____
    is also "Casual Friday."
    How should the employee dress? Why?
    A. Dress casually. The customers will understand that Casual Fridays are for casual dress, so they will not be upset.
    B. Business casual. An employee wants to assure customers that they handle business the way they dress, which means a smart, but comfortable look.

C. A little nicer than normally, but nothing too formal. This way they are still comfortable, but the customer knows that they are important too.
D. Dress in pajamas. Customers do not care what an employee wears as long as their presentation is good.

16. Professionally, what is the longest it should take someone to respond to a client email? How about a phone call?
    A. 45 minutes; 15 minutes
    B. 24 hours; 24 hours
    C. 48 hours; 24 hours
    D. 24 hours; 4 hours

16.____

17. Unlike social etiquette, office and business professionalism are PRIMARILY based on
    A. hierarchy and power
    B. personal relations between employees and customers
    C. common sense and courtesy
    D. both A and C

17.____

18. If something goes wrong during a customer interaction or presentation, what should you do?
    A. Clear your head, focus, and be cheerful and professional and act like nothing went wrong
    B. Take responsibility and take appropriate action
    C. Blame others for your technical difficulties
    D. Find a way to end the interaction as quickly as possible

18.____

19. What is the ultimate goal of customer service?
    A. Customer satisfaction
    B. Understanding customers
    C. Identify problems
    D. Improve product and service

19.____

20. Of the following, which is the BEST reason for employees and supervisors to frequently gauge customer satisfaction?
    A. No reason. One evaluation is enough.
    B. Because employees are not always honest about reporting customer satisfaction.
    C. They may have concerns or complaints that they have not voiced.
    D. Complaints do not always reach management.

20.____

21. Which of the following is TRUE of scope of influence?
    A. It is objective.
    B. Some have a larger scope of influence than others.
    C. Everyone has the same scope of influence.
    D. It is not relevant to customer service.

21.____

22. Which of the following techniques will create credibility in the minds of customers?
    A. Never admit being wrong. It undermines credibility.
    B. Demonstrate your human emotions. Whether you're angry or happy, let others see it.

22.____

C. Tell people what they want to hear even if it is not necessarily what you know to be true.
D. Become an expert about various factors in your profession. People will respect your knowledge.

23. You are in a "train the trainer" meeting about meeting customer expectations. As you talk in small groups after a short presentation, four people express very different statements about customer expectations.
Which one is CORRECT?
    A. "Wrong. Customer expectations are always changing."
    B. "Customer expectations rarely change."
    C. "Guys, all you really have to do is make a promise to solve customer problems. They forget after a while, even if you don't follow through."
    D. "Do not worry about what other companies are doing. We should focus on ourselves."

23.____

24. Of the following, which of the following is TRUE concerning customer service?
    A. Average customer service will always suffice.
    B. Customers lost through poor customer service are easy to replace.
    C. Organizations must provide excellent customer service or expect failure.
    D. None of the above

24.____

25. You are in a situation with a challenging customer.
How should you handle this situation?
    A. Make them respect and value your time.
    B. Avoid admitting any wrongdoing on your part.
    C. Find a solution and implement it.
    D. Do not show empathy.

25.____

KEY (CORRECT ANSWERS)

1. D
2. B
3. C
4. A
5. B

6. A
7. C
8. D
9. C
10. D

11. A
12. B
13. C
14. A
15. B

16. D
17. D
18. B
19. A
20. C

21. B
22. D
23. A
24. C
25. C

EXAMINATION SECTION
TEST 1

DIRECTIONS: Each question or incomplete statement is followed by several suggested answers or completions. Select the one that BEST answers the question or completes the statement. *PRINT THE LETTER OF THE CORRECT ANSWER IN THE SPACE AT THE RIGHT.*

1. In public agencies, communications should be based PRIMARILY on a
    A. two-way flow from the top down and from the bottom up, most of which should be given in writing to avoid ambiguity
    B. multi-direction flow among all levels and with outside persons
    C. rapid, internal one-way flow from the top down
    D. two-way flow of information, most of which should be given orally for purposes of clarity

    1.____

2. In some organizations, changes in policy or procedures are often communicated by word of mouth from supervisors to employees with no prior discussion or exchange of viewpoints with employees.
    This procedure often produces employee dissatisfaction CHIEFLY because
    A. information is mostly unusable since a considerable amount of time is required to transmit information
    B. lower-level supervisors tend to be excessively concerned with minor details
    C. management has failed to seek employees' advice before making changes
    D. valuable staff time is lost between decision-making and the implementation of decisions

    2.____

3. For good letter writing, you should try to visualize the person to whom you are writing, especially if you know him.
    Of the following rules, it is LEAST helpful in such visualization to think of
    A. the person's likes and dislikes, his concerns, and his needs
    B. what you would be likely to say if speaking in person
    C. what you would expect to be asked if speaking in person
    D. your official position in order to be certain that your words are proper

    3.____

4. One approach to good informal letter writing is to make letters and conversational.
    All of the following practices will usually help to do this EXCEPT:
    A. If possible, use a style which is similar to the style used when speaking
    B. Substitute phrases for single words (e.g., *at the present time* for *now*)
    C. Use contractions of words (e.g., *you're* for *you are*)
    D. Use ordinary vocabulary when possible

    4.____

5. All of the following rules will aid in producing clarity in report-writing EXCEPT:
   A. Give specific details or examples, if possible
   B. Keep related words close together in each sentence
   C. Present information in sequential order
   D. Put several thoughts or ideas in each paragraph

6. The one of the following statements about public relations which is MOST accurate is that
   A. in the long run, appearance gains better results than performance
   B. objectivity is decreased if outside public relations consultants are employed
   C. public relations is the responsibility of every employee
   D. public relations should be based on a formal publicity program

7. The form of communication which is usually considered to be MOST personally directed to the intended recipient is the
   A. brochure   B. film   C. letter   D. radio

8. In general, a document that presents an organization's views or opinions on a particular topic is MOST accurately known as a
   A. tear sheet   B. position paper
   C. flyer   D. journal

9. Assume that you have been asked to speak before an organization of persons who oppose a newly announced program in which you are involved. You feel tense about talking to this group.
   Which of the following rules generally would be MOST useful in gaining rapport when speaking before the audience?
   A. Impress them with your experience
   B. Stress all areas of disagreement
   C. Talk to the group as to one person
   D. Use formal grammar and language

10. An organization must have an effective public relations program since, at its best, public relations is a bridge to change.
    All of the following statements about communication and human behavior have validity EXCEPT:
    A. People are more likely to talk about controversial matters with like-minded people than with those holding other views
    B. The earlier an experience, the more powerful its effect since it influences how later experiences will be interpreted
    C. In periods of social tension, official sources gain increased believability
    D. Those who are already interested in a topic are the ones who are most open to receive new communications about it

11. An employee should be encouraged to talk easily and frankly when he is dealing with his supervisor.
    In order to encourage such free communication, it would be MOST appropriate for a supervisor to behave in a(n)
    A. sincere manner; assure the employee that you will deal with him honestly and openly
    B. official manner; you are a supervisor and must always act formally with subordinates
    C. investigative manner; you must probe and question to get to a basis of trust
    D. unemotional manner; the employee's emotions and background should play no part in your dealings with him

12. Research findings show that an increase in free communication within an agency GENERALLY results in which one of the following?
    A. Improved morale and productivity
    B. Increased promotional opportunities
    C. An increase in authority
    D. A spirit of honesty

13. Assume that you are a supervisor and your superiors have given you a new-type procedure to be followed.
    Before passing this information on to your subordinates, the one of the following actions that you should take FIRST is to
    A. ask your superiors to send out a memorandum to the entire staff
    B. clarify the procedure in your own mind
    C. set up a training course to provide instruction on the new procedure
    D. write a memorandum to your subordinates

14. Communication is necessary for an organization to be effective.
    The one of the following which is LEAST important for most communication systems is that
    A. messages are sent quickly and directly to the person who needs them to operate
    B. information should be conveyed understandably and accurately
    C. the method used to transmit information should be kept secret so that security can be maintained
    D. senders of messages must know how their messages are received and acted upon

15. Which one of the following is the CHIEF advantage of listening willingly to subordinates and encouraging them to talk freely and honestly?
    It
    A. reveals to supervisors the degree to which ideas that are passed down are accepted by subordinates
    B. reduces the participation of subordinates in the operation of the department
    C. encourages subordinates to try for promotion
    D. enables supervisors to learn more readily what the *grapevine* is saying

16. A supervisor may be informed through either oral or written reports. Which one of the following is an ADVANTAGE of using oral reports?
    A. There is no need for a formal record of the report.
    B. An exact duplicate of the report is not easily transmitted to others.
    C. A good oral report requires little time for preparation.
    D. An oral report involves two-way communication between a subordinate and his supervisor.

16._____

17. Of the following, the MOST important reason why supervisors should communicate effectively with the public is to
    A. improve the public's understanding of information that is important for them to know
    B. establish a friendly relationship
    C. obtain information about the kinds of people who come to the agency
    D. convince the public that services are adequate

17._____

18. Supervisors should generally NOT use phrases like *too hard*, *too easy*, and *a lot* PRINCIPALLY because such phrases
    A. may be offensive to some minority groups
    B. are too informal
    C. mean different things to different people
    D. are difficult to remember

18._____

19. The ability to communicate clearly and concisely is an important element in effective leadership.
    Which of the following statements about oral and written communication is GENERALLY true?
    A. Oral communication is more time-consuming.
    B. Written communication is more likely to be misinterpreted.
    C. Oral communication is useful only in emergencies.
    D. Written communication is useful mainly when giving information to fewer than twenty people.

19._____

20. Rumors can often have harmful and disruptive effects on an organization.
    Which one of the following is the BEST way to prevent rumors from becoming a problem?
    A. Refuse to act on rumors, thereby making them less believable.
    B. Increase the amount of information passed along by the *grapevine*.
    C. Distribute as much factual information as possible.
    D. Provide training in report writing.

20._____

21. Suppose that a subordinate asks you about a rumor he has heard. The rumor deals with a subject which your superiors consider *confidential*.
    Which of the following BEST describes how you should answer the subordinate? Tell

21._____

A. the subordinate that you don't make the rules and that he should speak to higher ranking officials
B. the subordinate that you will ask your superior for information
C. him only that you cannot comment on the matter
D. him the rumor is not true

22. Supervisors often find it difficult to *get their message across* when instructing newly appointed employees in their various duties.
The MAIN reason for this is generally that the
    A. duties of the employees have increased
    B. supervisor is often so expert in his area that he fails to see it from the learner's point of view
    C. supervisor adapts his instruction to the slowest learner in the group
    D. new employees are younger, less concerned with job security and more interested in fringe benefits

22.____

23. Assume that you are discussing a job problem with an employee under your supervision. During the discussion, you see that the man's eyes are turning away from you and that he is not paying attention.
In order to get the man's attention, you should FIRST
    A. ask him to look you in the eye
    B. talk to him about sports
    C. tell him he is being very rude
    D. change your tone of voice

23.____

24. As a supervisor, you may find it necessary to conduct meetings with your subordinates.
Of the following, which would be MOST helpful in assuring that a meeting accomplishes the purpose for which it was called?
    A. Give notice of the conclusions you would like to reach at the start of the meeting.
    B. Delay the start of the meeting until everyone is present.
    C. Write down points to be discussed in proper sequence.
    D. Make sure everyone is clear on whatever conclusions have been reached and on what must be done after the meeting.

24.____

25. Every supervisor will occasionally be called upon to deliver a reprimand to a subordinate. If done properly, this can greatly help an employee improve his performance.
Which one of the following is NOT a good practice to follow when giving a reprimand?
    A. Maintain your composure and temper
    B. Reprimand a subordinate in the presence of other employees so they can learn the same lesson
    C. Try to understand why the employee was not able to perform satisfactorily
    D. Let your knowledge of the man involved determine the exact nature of the reprimand

25.____

KEY (CORRECT ANSWERS)

1.	C		11.	A
2.	B		12.	A
3.	D		13.	B
4.	B		14.	C
5.	D		15.	A
6.	C		16.	D
7.	C		17.	A
8.	B		18.	C
9.	C		19.	B
10.	C		20.	C

21.	B
22.	B
23.	D
24.	D
25.	B

TEST 2

DIRECTIONS: Each question or incomplete statement is followed by several suggested answers or completions. Select the one that BEST answers the question or completes the statement. *PRINT THE LETTER OF THE CORRECT ANSWER IN THE SPACE AT THE RIGHT.*

1. Usually one thinks of communication as a single step, essentially that of transmitting an idea.
 Actually, however, this is only part of a total process, the FIRST step of which should be
 A. the prompt dissemination of the idea to those who may be affected by it
 B. motivating those affected to take the required action
 C. clarifying the idea in one's own mind
 D. deciding to whom the idea is to be communicated

 1._____

2. Research studies on patterns of informal communication have concluded that most individuals in a group tend to be passive recipients of news, while a few make it their business to spread it around in an organization.
 With this conclusion in mind, it would be MOST correct for the supervisor to attempt to identify these few individuals and
 A. give them the complete facts on important matters in advance of others
 B. inform the other subordinates of the identity of these few individuals so that their influence may be minimized
 C. keep them straight on the facts on important matters
 D. warn them to cease passing along any information to others

 2._____

3. The one of the following which is the PRINCIPAL advantage of making an oral report is that it
 A. affords an immediate opportunity for two-way communication between the subordinate and superior
 B. is an easy method for the superior to use in transmitting information to others of equal rank
 C. saves the time of all concerned
 D. permits more precise pinpointing of praise or blame by means of follow-up questions by the superior

 3._____

4. An agency may sometimes undertake a public relations program of a defensive nature.
 With reference to the use of defensive public relations, it would be MOST correct to state that it
 A. is bound to be ineffective since defensive statements, even though supported by factual data, can never hope to even partly overcome the effects of prior unfavorable attacks
 B. proves that the agency has failed to establish good relationships with newspapers, radio stations, or other means of publicity

 4._____

C. shows that the upper echelons of the agency have failed to develop sound public relations procedures and techniques
D. is sometimes required to aid morale by protecting the agency from unjustified criticism and misunderstanding of policies or procedures

5. Of the following factors which contribute to possible undesirable public attitudes towards an agency, the one which is MOST susceptible to being changed by the efforts of the individual employee in an organization is that
    A. enforcement of unpopular regulations as offended many individuals
    B. the organization itself has an unsatisfactory reputation
    C. the public is not interested in agency matters
    D. there are many errors in judgment committed by individual subordinates

5.____

6. It is not enough for an agency's services to be of a high quality; attention must also be given to the acceptability of these services to the general public.
This statement is GENERALLY
    A. *false*; a superior quality of service automatically wins public support
    B. *true*; the agency cannot generally progress beyond the understanding and support of the public
    C. *false*; the acceptance by the public of agency services determines their quality
    D. *true*; the agency is generally unable to engage in any effective enforcement activity without public support

6.____

7. Sustained agency participation in a program sponsored by a community organization is MOST justified when
    A. the achievement of agency objectives in some area depends partly on the activity of this organization
    B. the community organization is attempting to widen the base of participation in all community affairs
    C. the agency is uncertain as to what the community wants
    D. the agency is uncertain as to what the community wants

7.____

8. Of the following, the LEAST likely way in which a records system may serve a supervisor is in
    A. developing a sympathetic and cooperative public attitude toward the agency
    B. improving the quality of supervision by permitting a check on the accomplishment of subordinates
    C. permit a precise prediction of the exact incidences in specific categories for the following year
    D. helping to take the guesswork out of the distribution of the agency

8.____

9. Assuming that the *grapevine* in any organization is virtually indestructible, the one of the following which it is MOST important for management to understand is:
   A. What is being spread by means of the *grapevine* and the reason for spreading it
   B. What is being spread by means of the *grapevine* and how it is being spread
   C. Who is involved in spreading the information that is on the *grapevine*
   D. Why those who are involved in spreading the information are doing so

10. When the supervisor writes a report concerning an investigation to which he has been assigned, it should be LEAST intended to provide
    A. a permanent official record of relevant information gathered
    B. a summary of case findings limited to facts which tend to indicate the guilt of a suspect
    C. a statement of the facts on which higher authorities may base a corrective or disciplinary action
    D. other investigators with information so that they may continue with other phases of the investigation

11. In survey work, questionnaires rather than interviews are sometimes used. The one of the following which is a DISADVANTAGE of the questionnaire method as compared with the interview is the
    A. difficulty of accurately interpreting the results
    B. problem of maintaining anonymity of the participant
    C. fact that it is relatively uneconomical
    D. requirement of special training for the distribution of questionnaires

12. In his contacts with the public, an employee should attempt to create a good climate of support for his agency.
    This statement is GENERALLY
    A. *false*; such attempts are clearly beyond the scope of his responsibility
    B. *true*; employees of an agency who come in contact with the public have the opportunity to affect public relations
    C. *false*; such activity should be restricted to supervisors trained in public relations techniques
    D. *true*; the future expansion of the agency depends to a great extent on continued public support of the agency

13. The repeated use by a supervisor of a call for volunteers to get a job done is objectionable MAINLY because it
    A. may create a feeling of animosity between the volunteers and the non-volunteers
    B. may indicate that the supervisor is avoiding responsibility for making assignments which will be most productive
    C. is an indication that the supervisor is not familiar with the individual capabilities of his men
    D. is unfair to men who, for valid reasons, do not, or cannot volunteer

14. Of the following statements concerning subordinates' expressions to a supervisor of their opinions and feelings concerning work situations, the one which is MOST correct is that
    A. by listening and responding to such expressions the supervisor encourages the development of complaints
    B. the lack of such expressions should indicate to the supervisor that there is a high level of job satisfaction
    C. the more the supervisor listens to and responds to such expressions, the more he demonstrates lack of supervisory ability
    D. by listening and responding to such expressions, the supervisor will enable many subordinates to understand and solve their own problems on the job

15. In attempting to motivate employees, rewards are considered preferable to punishment PRIMARILY because
    A. punishment seldom has any effect on human behavior
    B. punishment usually results in decreased production
    C. supervisors find it difficult to punish
    D. rewards are more likely to result in willing cooperation

16. In an attempt to combat the low morale in his organization, a high level supervisor publicized an *open-door policy* to allow employees who wished to do so to come to him with their complaints.
    Which of the following is LEAST likely to account for the fact that no employee came in with a complaint?
    A. Employees are generally reluctant to go over the heads of their immediate supervisor.
    B. The employees did not feel that management would help them.
    C. The low morale was not due to complaints associated with the job.
    D. The employees felt that they had more to lose than to gain.

17. It is MOST desirable to use written instructions rather than oral instructions for a particular job when
    A. a mistake on the job will not be serious
    B. the job can be completed in a short time
    C. there is no need to explain the job minutely
    D. the job involves many details

18. If you receive a telephone call regarding a matter which your office does not handle, you should FIRST
    A. give the caller the telephone number of the proper office so that he can dial again
    B. offer to transfer the caller to the proper office
    C. suggest that the caller re-dial since he probably dialed incorrectly
    D. tell the caller he has reached the wrong office and then hang up

19. When you answer the telephone, the MOST important reason for identifying yourself and your organization is to
    A. give the caller time to collect his or her thoughts
    B. impress the caller with your courtesy
    C. inform the caller that he or she has reached the right number
    D. set a business-like tone at the beginning of the conversation

19.____

20. As soon as you pick up the phone, a very angry caller begins immediately to complain about city agencies and *red tape*. He says that he has been shifted to two or three different offices. It turs out that he is seeking information which is not immediately available to you. You believe, you know, however, where it can be found.
    Which of the following actions is the BEST one for you to take?
    A. To eliminate all confusion, suggest that the caller write the agency stating explicitly what he wants.
    B. Apologize by telling the caller how busy city agencies now are, but also tell him directly that you do not have the information he needs.
    C. Ask for the caller's telephone number and assure him you will call back after you have checked further.
    D. Give the caller the name and telephone number of the person who might be able to help, but explain that you are not positive he will get results/

20.____

21. Which of the following approaches usually provides the BEST communication in the objectives and values of a new program which is to be introduced?
    A. A general written description of the program by the program manager for review by those who share responsibility
    B. An effective verbal presentation by the program manager to those affected
    C. Development of the plan and operational approach in carrying out the program by the program manager assisted by his key subordinates
    D. Development of the plan by the program manager's supervisor

21.____

22. What is the BEST approach for introducing change?
    A
    A. combination of written and also verbal communication to all personnel affected by the change
    B. general bulletin to all personnel
    C. meeting pointing out all the values of the new approach
    D. written directive to key personnel

22.____

23. Of the following, committees are BEST used for
    A. advising the head of the organization
    B. improving functional work
    C. making executive decisions
    D. making specific planning decisions

23.____

24. An effective discussion leader is one who
    A. announces the problem and his preconceived solution at the start of the discussion
    B. guides and directs the discussion according to pre-arranged outline
    C. interrupts or corrects confused participants to save time
    D. permits anyone to say anything at any time

25. The human relations movement in management theory is basically concerned with
    A. counteracting employee unrest
    B. eliminating the *time and motion* man
    C. interrelationships among individuals in organizations
    D. the psychology of the worker

KEY (CORRECT ANSWERS)

1.	C	11.	A
2.	C	12.	B
3.	A	13.	B
4.	D	14.	D
5.	D	15.	D
6.	B	16.	C
7.	A	17.	D
8.	C	18.	B
9.	A	19.	C
10.	B	20.	C

21.	C
22.	A
23.	A
24.	B
25.	C

EXAMINATION SECTION
TEST 1

DIRECTIONS: Each question or incomplete statement is followed by several suggested answers or completions. Select the one that BEST answers the question or completes the statement. *PRINT THE LETTER OF THE CORRECT ANSWER IN THE SPACE AT THE RIGHT.*

1. A group member who starts out at the same level as other group members and is able to move into a leadership position within that group would be described as what kind of a leader? 1.____
    A. Autocratic   B. Democratic   C. Emergent   D. Informal

2. Your boss is only effective as the leader of your department when you and your coworkers are motivated experts on the topic at hand. If any of you do not really have expertise in a given field, his leadership falters somewhat. What type of leader is your boss? 2.____
    A. Laissez-faire   B. Technical   C. Democratic   D. Autocratic

3. If a leader is in charge of an inexperienced group that does not have the appropriate information and proficiency to successfully complete a task, which of the following approaches should the leader use in order for success to follow within the group? 3.____
    A. Yelling   B. Delegating   C. Participating   D. Selling

4. If you are a democratic leader, which of the following styles will be reflective of your leadership technique? 4.____
    A. Participating   B. Telling   C. Yelling   D. Delegating

5. In producing equality in group member participation, which of the following should a leader NOT do? 5.____
    A. Make a statement or ask a question after each person in the group has said something
    B. Avoid taking a position during disagreements
    C. Limit comments to specific individuals within the group
    D. Control dominating speakers

6. Social capital is BEST defined as 6.____
    A. social connections that help us make more money
    B. social connections that improve our lives
    C. a type of connection that experts believe is becoming more common in Europe than the United States.
    D. none of the above

7. Communication is not simply sending a message. It is creating true 7.____
    A. connectivity   B. understanding
    C. empathy   D. power

8. Of the following, which is NOT a part of the speech communication process?
   A. Feedback
   B. Central idea
   C. Interference
   D. Ethics

9. You are leading a meeting and afterwards your colleagues tell you they didn't quite understand what you were communicating verbally and nonverbally to them. Which part of the communication process do you need to work on?
   A. Channel
   B. Main idea
   C. Message
   D. Specific purpose

10. If nonverbal messages contradict verbal symbols, you are sending what kind of message to your public?
    A. Clear
    B. Mixed
    C. Controversial
    D. Negative

11. Which of the following would a public speaker use to deliver verbal symbols?
    A. Words
    B. Gestures
    C. Tone
    D. Facial expression

12. You are in the process of taking a course on interacting with the public. Your instructor starts talking about "the pathway" used to transmit a message. He explains that "the pathway" is better known as a
    A. link   B. loop   C. transmitter   D. channel

13. You finish an informational meeting with members of a community concerning a new park that will be built nearby. Afterwards, you are seeking feedback from them. Which of the following would NOT be a form of helpful feedback to you?
    A. Listeners raise their hands to point out a mistake
    B. Videotape the presentation
    C. Have colleagues and/or friends critique your presentation
    D. Hand out evaluation forms to listeners and have them fill it out after the presentation

14. Many public speaking experts have often repeated the famous quote, "A yawn is a silent _____," which references the quality of engagement within a presentation.
    A. rudeness   B. insult   C. shout   D. protest

15. If a child is running around during your speech and making a lot of noise, what type of interference would that be?
    A. Situational   B. External   C. Internal   D. Intentional

16. According to multiple recent surveys, of the five biggest mistakes that speakers make during a presentation, which one is the WORST?
    A. Being poorly prepared
    B. Trying to cover too much in one speech
    C. Failing to tailor a speech to the needs and interests of the audience
    D. Being boring

17. One of your colleagues has been asked to lead a meeting, and she confides in you that she suffers from excessive stage fright. Which of the following areas should you advise her to focus on to prevent her fear?
    A. Preparation
    B. Self-confidence
    C. Experience
    D. Sense of humor

17.____

18. When interacting with the public, which of the following elements should you NEVER imagine before engaging in public speaking?
    A. Effective delivery
    B. Nervousness
    C. Possibility of failure
    D. Success

18.____

19. A spokesperson is giving a speech to community members and you are evaluating him. You notice he tends to focus too much on himself and not enough on his audience. What is one piece of advice you can give him so he can shift his focus more to his audience?
    A. Change his amount of eye contact
    B. Work on facial expressions
    C. Alter his style of speaking
    D. All of the above

19.____

20. Most experts agree that the best way to eliminate excess energy would be to do all of the following EXCEPT
    A. using visual aids
    B. gripping the lectern
    C. walking to the right and left occasionally
    D. making gestures

20.____

21. A woman has lived in Newville her whole life. Recently, the Newville public works department made a policy change that angered her since it completely rearranged her schedule. She calls you on the phone and displays her displeasure with your department's recent policy change. What is the FIRST response you should have toward her?
    A. Interrupt her to say you cannot discuss the situation until she calms down
    B. Apologize to her that she has been negatively affected by the public works department
    C. Listen to her and demonstrate comprehension of her situation and why she was upset by your department's action
    D. Give her a detailed explanation of the reasons for the policy change

21.____

22. Which of the following is generally TRUE regarding public opinion?
    A. It is hard to move people toward a strong opinion on anything
    B. It is easy to move people toward a strong opinion on anything
    C. Most public relations are devoted to repairing negative public opinion about individuals
    D. It is easier than previously thought to move people away from an opinion they hold

22.____

23. Influencing a community member's attitude really comes down to which of the following?
    A. Journalism
    B. Public relations
    C. Social psychology
    D. Social action groups

23.____

24. If you attend a town hall meeting in which community members will bring up issues that require you to explain why your organization made the decisions it made, you will need to persuade them using evidence that is virtually indisputable. Which type of evidence should you stick to when explaining answers to the public?
    A. Facts
    B. Personal experience
    C. Emotions
    D. Using what appeals to the target public

25. In the last decade, especially after all the organizational and governmental scandals, public institutions must do which of the following in order to be successful?
    A. Work hard to earn and sustain favorable public opinion
    B. Trust the instincts expressed by the general public
    C. Be cognizant of the media's power
    D. Place the needs of the executives ahead of the needs of the public and other constituents

KEY (CORRECT ANSWERS)

1.	C	11.	A
2.	A	12.	D
3.	B	13.	A
4.	D	14.	C
5.	A	15.	B
6.	B	16.	C
7.	B	17.	A
8.	D	18.	B
9.	C	19.	D
10.	B	20.	B

21. C
22. D
23. B
24. A
25. A

TEST 2

DIRECTIONS: Each question or incomplete statement is followed by several suggested answers or completions. Select the one that BEST answers the question or completes the statement. *PRINT THE LETTER OF THE CORRECT ANSWER IN THE SPACE AT THE RIGHT.*

1. Unique attributes of the Internet that people can enjoy include all of the following EXCEPT
    A. immediacy
    B. low cost
    C. pervasiveness
    D. value for building one-to-one human relationships

    1.____

2. Which of the following is a reason that social media can be more effective than traditional means of advertising and communication?
    A. When someone mentions your brand in social media, there is much more potential for other people to notice
    B. It is easier to decipher tone and purpose through Twitter or Facebook than through personal communication
    C. Most of the people who would be interested in your brand or service are comfortable and familiar with using social media
    D. Almost anyone can step into a media relations role if primarily using social media, because it is easy to communicate effectively through social media platforms

    2.____

3. You are tasked with building publicity for the upcoming reveal of a new art installation in the town you work in. Your boss tells you to contact journalists, reporters and bloggers to help spread the word. Which of the following would be the MOST effective way of getting the media to help build coverage?
    A. Send out a mass e-mail to any media members in the area detailing the art installation and why you need coverage for it
    B. Call each media outlet and find out who would most likely cover and build publicity for your project. Then reach out to them either face-to-face or through a phone call
    C. Using Twitter, tweet at the media members and introduce yourself and your art installation and ask them to help spread the word
    D. None of the above

    3.____

4. When using written communication, which of the following is a MAJOR challenge of writing to listeners?
    A. Providing lots of statistics
    B. Grabbing the attention of the listener quickly
    C. Providing information that is easily reviewed
    D. Presenting lots of incidentals

    4.____

5. In order to communicate well in writing, which of the following pieces of advice sounds good but doesn't actually help you?
   A. Write material for all audiences rather than focusing on one
   B. Think before writing
   C. Write simply and with clarity
   D. Write and rewrite until you have a polished, finished product

6. You send out a public newsletter that details a project that your team is currently working on. One week later, an employee on your team tells you she has received multiple phone calls from confused constituents claiming that the newsletter's readability was low. When you send out a corrected newsletter, you need to make sure that your communication is easy to
   A. read   B. hear   C. edit   D. comprehend

7. You work for a biomedical company as a public outreach advocate. One day, an exciting e-mail circulates internally that states one of your scientists has discovered a cure for leukemia and your supervisor tasks you with writing the release. When writing the release, the newsworthy element inherent in the story is
   A. oddity   B. conflict   C. impact   D. proximity

8. When communicating with the public through the Internet, news releases
   A. should not be sent via e-mail
   B. should be succinct
   C. should be sent via "snail mail"
   D. none of the above

9. What is the MAJOR advantage of organizational publications? Their ability to
   A. give sponsoring organizations a means of uncontrolled communications
   B. deliver specific, detailed information to narrowly defined target publics
   C. avoid the problems typically associated with two-way media
   D. provide a revenue source for sponsoring organizations

10. You are confronted by a question from a reporter that you do not know the answer to. What should you do?
    A. Give them other information you are certain is right
    B. Tell them that information is "off the record" and will be distributed later
    C. Say "no comment" rather than look like you're uninformed
    D. Admit that you don't know but promise to provide the information later

11. Often times, an organization will run situation analysis before they share information with the public. Which one of these "internal factors" is usually associated with a situational analysis?
    A. A communication audit
    B. Community focus groups
    C. A list of media contacts
    D. Strategy suggestions

12. When you are hired, your first task is to start a process of identifying who are involved and affected by a situation central to your organization. This process is MOST commonly referred to as a(n)
    A. situation interview
    B. communication audit
    C. exploratory survey
    D. stakeholder analysis

12.____

13. Once a public outreach plan is in the summative evaluation phase, which of the following is generally associated with it?
    A. Impact
    B. Implementation
    C. Attitude change
    D. Preparation

13.____

14. Which of the following Internet-related challenges is MOST significant in the public relations field?
    A. Finding stable, cost-effective internet provides
    B. Representing clients using new social media environments
    C. Staying abreast of changing technology
    D. Training staff to use social media

14.____

15. Which of the following BEST defines a public issue? Any
    A. problem that brings a public lawsuit
    B. concern that is of mutual distress to competitors
    C. issue that is of mutual concern to an organization and its stakeholders
    D. problem that is not a concern to an organization and/or one of its stakeholders

15.____

16. A handful of people are posting misleading and/or negative information about your organization. What is the MOST proactive approach to handling this situation?
    A. Buy up enough shares in the site where the negative posts are, and prevent those users from posting again
    B. Post anonymous comments on the sites to help combat the negativity
    C. Prepare news releases that discredit the inaccuracies
    D. Make policy changes to address complaints highlighted on the sites

16.____

17. Your supervisor has recently asked you to review present and future realities for interacting with the public. Why is it important to continually review these?
    A. It helps develop your vision statement
    B. It helps interpret trends for management
    C. It helps construe the organization's business plan
    D. To know what path the company should pursue

17.____

18. You are the community relations director for the public water utility plant that has been the focus of a group of activists who are opposed to the addition of fluoride to drinking water. These objectors are not only at the plant each day, but they are also very active on social media inciting negativity towards the practice. As the director of the plant, you have overwhelming evidence that contradicts what the protestors are arguing. You want to combat their social media with your own internet plan. Which of the following is the MOST appropriate action for you to take? 18.____
    A. Use utility employees to write the blog, posing as healthcare professionals
    B. Reach out to medical professionals to volunteer to tweet and message community members under their own identities, but with no reference to the utility company
    C. Write a blog yourself, identifying yourself as an employee, and quote the scientific opinions of a variety of sources
    D. Pay for medical professionals to respond through the internet, identifying the utility as their sponsor, but without disclosing the compensation

19. You have recently completed an advertising campaign to help assuage the anger of the community at changes in the upcoming summer program for the city. Which of the following measurements would be MOST effective for evaluating the campaign's impact on audience attitude? 19.____
    A. A content analysis of media coverage
    B. Studying blog postings about the issue
    C. Analyzing pre- and post-numbers of people signed up for the summer programs
    D. Conducting a pre- and post-analysis of public opinions

20. In order to measure how policy changes will affect the public, you recommend that your supervisors first run a focus group for research. They like the idea, but want you to be in charge of running the group. Which of the following should you keep in mind as you form the focus group? 20.____
    A. Participants need to be randomly selected
    B. Make sure participants are radically different from one another so you get a range of opinions
    C. Include at least seven or more people in the group. Otherwise, the sample is too small to draw any conclusions.
    D. Formulate a research plan and use it as a script so you can make sure the results are ones that will work for you and your supervisors

21. The public university has recently come under fire for not offering enough tuition savings options for students. You have been hired to help promote the programs they offer including new savings programs. What is the MOST appropriate first step for you to take? 21.____
    A. Research pricing and development costs for the services
    B. Develop a survey to discover which factors impact families' savings
    C. Conduct a situation analysis to gain better understanding of the issues
    D. Hold a focus group to determine which messages would be most effective for your program

5 (#2)

22. After receiving feedback from the public on a new program, you are concerned the results have been tainted by courtesy bias. You plan on sending out a new questionnaire, but you need to make sure the bias is discouraged in it. Which of the following techniques will be MOST effective at decreasing the partiality?
    A. Make questionnaire responses confidential
    B. Employ an outside firm to run the survey
    C. Offer a larger range of responses in the survey
    D. Both "A" and "C"

22.____

23. You have just relocated from Omaha, Nebraska to a branch in Chicago, Illinois. In order to communicate well while in Chicago, you must remember that
    A. most publics have the same needs
    B. all publics are most interested only in technology you are using
    C. each audience has its own special needs and require different types of communication
    D. all audiences' needs overlap

23.____

24. Recently, the Parks and Recreation Department has come under fire because it has been accused of too much marketing and not enough public relations. Which of the following, if true, would lend credibility to these accusations?
    A. Employees are focused on signing citizens up for as many different camps and activities available over the summer as possible
    B. Management consistently tries to send appreciation gifts to members of the community when they have volunteered or attending an activity sponsored by the Park district
    C. Weekly meetings are held to determine how to best improve the Park district's image as it relates to consumers
    D. Parks and Recreation is primarily focused on making sure the public enjoys their activities and trusts them to put on educational programs for the children

24.____

25. During your speech, a community member stands up and accuses you of "spinning" a story. Which of the following BEST describes their accusation?
    A. You are relating a message through an agreed-upon ethical practice within the public relations community
    B. You are twisting a message to create performance where there is none
    C. You are trying to preserve hard-earned credibility
    D. You are providing the media with balanced and accurate information

25.____

KEY (CORRECT ANSWERS)

1.	D		11.	A
2.	A		12.	D
3.	C		13.	A
4.	B		14.	C
5.	D		15.	C
6.	D		16.	B
7.	C		17.	A
8.	B		18.	C
9.	B		19.	D
10.	D		20.	A

21.	C
22.	D
23.	C
24.	A
25.	B

TEST 3

DIRECTIONS: Each question or incomplete statement is followed by several suggested answers or completions. Select the one that BEST answers the question or completes the statement. *PRINT THE LETTER OF THE CORRECT ANSWER IN THE SPACE AT THE RIGHT.*

1. In order to be successful in relating to the public, all of the following are vital EXCEPT
   A. performance
   B. relationship building
   C. formal education
   D. diversity of experience

   1.____

2. Which of the following is TRUE of communicating well regarding public relations experts?
   A. It will differentiate you and your role from others with special skills in the organization you work for
   B. It should be handled delicately in order to avoid upsetting stakeholders
   C. It is not as important as looking fashionable
   D. It is less important than understanding bureaucratic peculiarities

   2.____

3. You are critiquing a staffer who will lead an important meeting in two days and you note that she keeps using words that are steeped with connotation. You tell her to be careful of these words. Why?
   A. They transmit meaning too clearly, and you always want to leave wiggle room in your meaning
   B. They transmit the dictionary definition of a word that makes for a boring presentation
   C. They transmit meaning with an emotional overtone that could lead to misunderstanding in an overall message
   D. They lend themselves to stereotyping

   3.____

4. If you are trying to avoid biasing your intended audience, which of the following factors could help with that?
   A. Symbols
   B. Objective reporting by media
   C. Semantics
   D. Peers

   4.____

5. Of the following, which trait is MOST desirable when working with the public?
   A. Having the "gift for gab"
   B. Being an elite strategist
   C. Being able to leap organizational boundaries
   D. Performing well, especially in crises

   5.____

6. Which of the following areas is likely to see continual growth in the practice of public relations?
   A. Healthcare
   B. Social media
   C. Law enforcement
   D. None of the above

   6.____

47

7. What is the MOST commonly used public relations tactic?
   A. A news release
   B. A special event
   C. A PSA (public service announcement)
   D. A full feature news article

8. You have just been assigned to help with a new advertising campaign that will promote the new services offered by your organization. One major component of the new campaign will focus on publicity through photographs. Knowing you need to get this part of the project right, which of the following is the BEST tip to remember when taking PR photos?
   A. Don't use action shots because they usually wind up blurry
   B. Make sure there is good contrast and sharp detail
   C. Ensure that the product/services are the biggest thing(s) in the photo
   D. Photograph multiple people rather than only one

9. Which of the following situations would merit holding a press conference?
   A. When a corporation is restructured
   B. When a new public relations employee has been hired
   C. When information is of minor relevance to a specific audience
   D. When there is a new product to be released

10. On average, how long should an announcement to the public last on the radio?
    A. 2 minutes   B. 20 seconds   C. 1 minute   D. 10 seconds

11. In educating the public, you need to develop a PR plan and analyze each situation that could arise. Which of the following should NOT be a part of the analysis?
    A. Research
    B. Message crafting
    C. Creating a problem statement
    D. Asking the 5 W's and the H

12. You are in charge of promoting an event in the near future, but social media is unavailable to you at this time. Which of the following is the BEST way to get your message out to the media and, therefore, the public?
    A. An Op-Ed piece in the local newspaper
    B. A press conference
    C. A newsletter
    D. A news release

13. In the past few months, you and your colleagues have been accused of "doublespeak". Which of the following excerpts from presentations you have used could you defend and explain why it would NOT be an example of "doublespeak"?
    A. You called combat "fighting"
    B. Fred referred to genocide as "ethnic cleansing"
    C. Your boss referred to recent layoffs as "downsizing"
    D. Susie called the janitor a "custodial engineer"

14. In relating to the public, which of the following reflects key words in defining modern day PR?
    A. Deliberate, public interest, management function
    B. Persuasive, manipulative, improvisation
    C. Management, technical, flexible
    D. Influential, creative, evaluative

15. How is educating and relating to the public different from being a journalist, marketing agent, or advertiser?
    A. It is more focused on advocacy
    B. It is about getting "free" press coverage
    C. It is about building relationships with various demographics
    D. All of the above

16. Of the following, what is the BEST tactic for learning employee attitudes?
    A. Internal communications audit
    B. Research
    C. Conference meeting
    D. Both A and B

17. When releasing news to the public, you should make sure it reads at a _____-grade reading level.
    A. 5th   B. 12th   C. 9th   D. 7th

18. If you are using a euphemism that actually changes the meaning/impact of a concept you are trying to relay, what is that called?
    A. Insider language
    B. Doublespeak
    C. Stylizing
    D. Plagiarism

19. Which of the following should be included in a public relations campaign if you want to ensure people will hear, understand, and believe your message?
    A. Repetition
    B. Imagery
    C. Thoroughness
    D. Acceptance

20. In PR, what is it called when you track coverage and compare it over a period of time?
    A. Bookmarking
    B. Benchmarking
    C. Comparison analysis
    D. Correspondence

21. What is a baseline study PRIMARILY used for?
    A. To determine changes in audience perception and attitude
    B. To figure out how well your company is doing in the marketplace compared to your competitors
    C. To find out the cost of buying space taken up by a particular article if that article is an advertisement
    D. None of the above

22. Of the following people, who would BEST be considered a modern role model for successful public relations?
    A. Phineas T. Barnum (Barnum and Bailey)
    B. Ivy Lee
    C. Andrew Jackson
    D. Sir Walter Raleigh

23. If your organization has recently participated in a "publicity stunt," what type of PR strategy have you just used?
    A. Community
    B. Lobbying
    C. News management
    D. Crisis management

24. You tell your supervisor that you want to start using video press releases. When he presses you to explain why, you tell him that you want to take advantage of the fact that
    A. many news agencies don't review them ahead of broadcasting
    B. most reporters hired to create them have contacts within the industry
    C. they cover stories that some local news organizations cannot
    D. the production value may be better than those at local stations

25. A _____ is a type of news leak in which the source reveals large policy changes are on the table.
    A. disclosure   B. hook   C. exclusive   D. trial balloon

KEY (CORRECT ANSWERS)

1. C
2. B
3. C
4. B
5. D

6. B
7. A
8. B
9. D
10. C

11. B
12. D
13. A
14. A
15. D

16. D
17. C
18. B
19. A
20. B

21. A
22. B
23. C
24. C
25. D

TEST 4

DIRECTIONS: Each question or incomplete statement is followed by several suggested answers or completions. Select the one that BEST answers the question or completes the statement. *PRINT THE LETTER OF THE CORRECT ANSWER IN THE SPACE AT THE RIGHT.*

1. The Facial Feedback Hypothesis is a popular nonverbal theory that is BEST defined as
    A. people mirroring each other's facial expressions
    B. emotions leading to certain facial expressions
    C. facial expression can lead to the experience of certain emotions
    D. looking into a mirror while making a facial expression can cause one to change their facial expression

1.____

2. Of the following, which is NOT recognized as a function of smiling?
    A. It provides feedback.
    B. It signals disinterest.
    C. It helps establish rapport.
    D. It signals attentiveness.

2.____

3. When facial expressions are limited by cultural expectations, that is referred to as
    A. display rules
    B. syntactic displays
    C. adaptors
    D. interaction intensification

3.____

4. Of the following, which is recognized as part of the six basic emotions across cultures globally?
    A. Guilt
    B. Happiness
    C. Fear
    D. Both B and C

4.____

5. Which kinds of communication scenarios are more likely to see leadership roles develop from?
    A. Small group
    B. Intrapersonal communication
    C. Face-to-face public communication
    D. Text messaging

5.____

6. Which of the following highlights the key difference between small group communication and organizational communication?
    A. Feedback is easier and more immediate in organizational.
    B. Communication is more informal in small group communication.
    C. The message is easier to adapt to the specific needs of the receiver in organizational communication.
    D. People are more spread out in small group communication.

6.____

7. Which of the following would be an example of mediated communication?
    A. A principal addresses the student body in a speech.
    B. Two friends communicate while they work together in class.
    C. An employee texts his coworkers to see if they want to hang out after work.
    D. Three friends joke with one another while attending a concert.

7.____

8. Which of the following is FALSE concerning the way interpersonal relationships can affect us physically?
   A. Without interpersonal relationships, we can become sick
   B. These interpersonal relationships are necessary for humans; according to most research, humans raised in isolation are less healthy than those raised with others
   C. Humans are not the only mammals that need relationships in order to survive and thrive
   D. Interpersonal relationships are necessary until about age 12, but not later in adulthood

9. Which of the following is a characteristic of public relationships as they compare to private relationships?
   A. Intrinsic rewards
   B. Normative rules
   C. Use of particularistic knowledge
   D. Small number of intimates

10. When someone asks how you know they were angry, it is likely they fall into which style of facial expressions?
    A. Withholder
    B. Revealer
    C. Frozen-affect expressor
    D. Unwitting expressor

11. The theory of expectancy violations is BEST defined as
    A. nonverbal behavior reciprocated based primarily on positive or negative valence and the perceived reward value of the other person
    B. the process of intimacy exchange within a dyad relationship
    C. a social rule that says we should repay in kind what another has provided us
    D. none of the above

12. If an employee has a very good idea of what is and is not socially acceptable in any given situation, which kind of linguistic competence is she strong in?
    A. Phonemic   B. Syntactic   C. Pragmatic   D. Semantic

13. Which of the following would NOT be considered sexist language?
    A. Although a girl, Sonia is very brave.
    B. A gorgeous model, Johnny also likes to use his surfboard on the weekends.
    C. Jimmy's brother is a male nurse.
    D. None; all are considered to be sexist.

14. What is it called when individual experience, and NOT conventional agreement, creates meaning?
    A. Small talk communication
    B. Denotative meaning
    C. Connotative meaning
    D. Self-reflexive communication

15. Which of the following kinds of communication do students spend the MOST time engaged in?
    A. Listening   B. Writing   C. Reading   D. Speaking

16. Which of the following would be evidence of active listening?
    A. Maintain eye contact
    B. Nodding and making eye contact
    C. Asking for clarification
    D. All of the above

17. When listening in an evaluative context, which of the following must be done for it to be considered successful?
    A. Precisely disseminate stimuli in a message
    B. Comprehend the intended meaning of a message
    C. Make critical assessments of the accuracy of the facts in a message
    D. All of the above

18. A friend visits one day and tells you she thinks her husband is cheating on her with his ex-wife. She tells you she doesn't know what to do because she can't imagine living without him. If you wanted to paraphrase, which of the following BEST exemplifies that?
    A. "You are feeling insecure because you don't have a very good relationship with your husband."
    B. "You're afraid your husband is seeing his ex-wife behind your back; you don't know what to do; and you can't live without him."
    C. "You're afraid that your husband may still have feelings for his ex-wife and you're afraid you'll lose him."
    D. "Don't worry; his ex-wife is not back with him. You're just being paranoid."

19. When we form impressions of others, when might the recency effect impact our assessments? If we
    A. focus on our own feelings instead of the feelings of others
    B. are motivated to be more accurate or expect to be held accountable for our own perceptions
    C. engage in self-monitoring of our behaviors
    D. employ the discounting rule

20. Which of the following BEST defines a "modal self"?
    A. The ideal person for a social order
    B. A person who does not go to extremes
    C. The kind of self valued in the 20th century but not the 21st century
    D. The person who monitors his own behavior in social situations

21. Which of the following is TRUE of today's society?
    A. People are less selfish than they have ever been.
    B. People spend most of their time trying to be a single, unitary self.
    C. People have many short-lived relationships leading to their notions of themselves changing easily.
    D. People try to be frugal, honorable, and self-sacrificing.

22. A man's childhood consisted of a dismissing attachment style. Which of the following behaviors will he MOST likely exhibit as an adult?
    A. Anxiousness and ambivalence
    B. Obsessive friendliness and dependence
    C. Autonomy and distance from others
    D. Rhetorical sensitivity

23. When practicing self-disclosure, which of the following is a good rule of thumb?
    A. Be sure to disclose more than your partner
    B. Reserve your most important disclosures for people you know well
    C. Ignore the style of disclosure; the only thing that is important is content
    D. All of the above

24. During your first meeting as project leader, you approach your group and inform them that John will serve as your assistant project leader. He will be responsible for chairing team meetings and establishing the agenda. When John is given this formal leadership position, what type of power does he have over the other members of the project?
    A. Legitimate   B. Reward   C. Expert   D. Punishment

25. If you bring an employee to lead a project because she is knowledgeable and skilled in the area the project focuses on, what type of power does she possess?
    A. Legitimate   B. Reward   C. Referent   D. Expert

KEY (CORRECT ANSWERS)

1. C
2. B
3. A
4. D
5. A

6. B
7. C
8. D
9. B
10. D

11. A
12. C
13. D
14. C
15. A

16. D
17. C
18. B
19. D
20. A

21. C
22. C
23. B
24. A
25. D

EXAMINATION SECTION
TEST 1

DIRECTIONS: Each question or incomplete statement is followed by several suggested answers or completions. Select the one that BEST answers the question or completes the statement. *PRINT THE LETTER OF THE CORRECT ANSWER IN THE SPACE AT THE RIGHT.*

1. Which of the following are covered under the definition of customer service?
   A. A positive environment set up to efficiently handle customer requests
   B. Infrastructure designed to distribute merchandise in a timely fashion
   C. Employees filling distinct roles to meet customer needs
   D. All of the above

   1.____

2. An organization that has a clearly established customer service approach can distinguish itself from competitors. This is referred to as the organization's
   A. customer prioritization　　　B. service culture
   C. imagineering　　　　　　　　D. none of the above

   2.____

3. The physical space of a hospitality setting is MOST commonly referred to as the
   A. customer landscape　　　　B. business policy
   C. servicescape　　　　　　　　D. arena of service

   3.____

4. When dealing with a customer, one must be knowledgeable, capable and enthusiastic when delivering products and/or services and it must be done in a manner that satisfies
   A. both identified and unidentified needs
   B. local and global competition
   C. quality and quantity of goods/services
   D. all demands of the customer

   4.____

5. Employees at the center learn at their orientation that services are inseparable because service quality and customer satisfaction are largely dependent on which of the following?
   A. Interactions between employees and customers
   B. Uniform offerings for individuals
   C. Establishing patents for individual services
   D. All of the above

   5.____

6. An organization with a strong customer service culture
   A. allows employees to use their own initiative to solve customer problems
   B. has policies that allow employees to easily please customers
   C. provides extensive customer service training for employees
   D. all of the above

   6.____

7. Which of the following is TRUE of customer contact through electronic mail? 7.____
   A. Be sure to use all caps for important aspects of the e-mail
   B. State the purpose of the message clearly
   C. Do not feel the need to respond immediately
   D. Include lengthy descriptions in the body of the e-mail

8. A clerk is speaking to residents at a zoning committee meeting and uses the 8.____
   word "coulda" instead of "could have" in his presentation.
   This is an example of
   A. good enunciation   B. poor tone
   C. poor enunciation   D. proper pitch

9. An employee is delivering a presentation to parents about the benefits of children 9.____
   joining summer camps when someone complains that the employee's changing
   pitch makes it hard to hear what he is saying and that he needs to fix it.
   What does the parent mean by fixing his pitch?
   The employee needs to
   A. keep his voice from going too high or too low
   B. keep his voice from getting too soft or too loud
   C. keep his attitude towards certain subjects in check
   D. make sure his words are clearly spoken and not garbled

10. A clerk recently moved from answering phone calls every day to working 10.____
    face-to-face with residents.
    Which of the following will help her be most successful when transferring from
    phone to personal communication?
    A. Focus on sharing only positive information
    B. Speak more authoritatively
    C. Maintain a more casual tone and familiarity with residents
    D. Positive communication through eye contact and body language

11. Talking via telephone 11.____
    A. is less personal than sending an e-mail message
    B. is a poor way to reach most residents
    C. can allow residents to receive instant feedback
    D. is not popular within public services

12. An employee is in charge of calling local homeowners to tell them about 12.____
    upcoming activities, and more often than not she needs to leave a voicemail.
    Which of the following is the MOST effective way to leave voicemails?
    A. Be courteous
    B. Provide the appropriate information
    C. Contain lengthy details
    D. Both A and B

13. You are dealing with a parent who is upset about a miscommunication related to her child's application for an activity. Which of the following would be LEAST frustrating for the parent to hear from you?
    A. "I don't know. I will do my best."
    B. "Let me see what I can do for you."
    C. "I apologize, but you will have to…"
    D. "Oh, my manager should be able to help you, but he's not in right now."

14. If a part-time assistant employee should need to apologize to customers, which of the following should he NOT do when apologizing?
    A. Apologize right away
    B. Be sincere in his apology
    C. Make the apology personal
    D. Offer an official apology from the department

15. If a clerk's office is looking to improve its processes to increase community satisfaction, feedback received should be each of the following EXCEPT
    A. centered on internal customers
    B. ongoing
    C. available internally to everyone from employees to supervisors
    D. focused on a limited number of indicators

16. A member of the community has identified a flaw in one of the policies regarding town hall meetings. Now that the problem has been identified, all of the following should be steps toward resolving the issue EXCEPT
    A. following up on the problem resolution
    B. making whatever promises are necessary
    C. listening and responding to all complaints
    D. providing the resident with whatever was originally requested

17. When looking to achieve the best results as someone who interacts with the public, one should always strive to represent
    A. the entire organization   B. the customer
    C. the department   D. their direct supervisor

18. Approximately how long does it take a person on hold to become annoyed?
    A. 1 minute   B. 40 seconds   C. 20 seconds   D. 2 minutes

19. If an employee answers the phone and is asked to transfer the call to a co-worker, which of the following would be the MOST appropriate response?
    A. "She isn't in right now, so I'll have to take a message."
    B. "She's still at lunch. Can I take a message?"
    C. "She should be back soon. Could you call back in 15 minutes?"
    D. "Let me transfer you. If she's not in, please leave a message and she will return your call."

20. A public employee has been specifically assigned to deal with public complaints because he is remarkably skilled at dealing with residents. Which of the following mentalities would explain why the employee is so effective at dealing with residents?
    A. They always cave in to whatever demands the residents make
    B. They effectively manage residents' expectations
    C. They always sincerely apologize no matter who is at fault
    D. Both A and C

21. When dealing with a frustrated customer, which of the following practices should an employee avoid?
    A. Immediately offer a solution to their problem
    B. Soothe the customer's frustration first
    C. Remain positive and non-confrontational with the customer
    D. Let the customer vent and feel like they've shared their feelings accurately

22. The town clerk's office in Avondale is highly rated by town residents. When surveyed, residents of Avondale claim that their town clerks always have such great customer service.
    Of the customer service techniques listed below, which one is MOST likely the reason for such high ratings?
    A. When dealing with abusive residents, Avondale clerks always hang up on them
    B. Clerks in Avondale have a readied list of solutions to resident problems, so they are able to offer personalized solutions right away
    C. Avondale clerks always follow up with residents who call or come in
    D. Clerks always look customers in the eye even when they are frustrated and upset

23. If a parent was told there would be space in a day camp for all of her children, and only two of them ended up being placed together, which of the following actions would be PROPER for a parks employee to take?
    A. Offer a sincere apology and attempt to fix the problem
    B. Promise the parent that all her children will be together even if it means dropping other children from the camp
    C. Explain the Parks Department policy regarding camp sign-up and tell the parent to contact a manager for further explanation
    D. Tell the parent she needs to speak to someone with more authority

24. If a person has a hearing impairment, which of the following practical solutions could a clerk have in place to help them?
    A. Reading a description of policy to the person
    B. Write a note to answer a question they have
    C. Read the words communicated by the person's "communication board"
    D. Assist the person in maneuvering through the physical space of the office

25. When dealing with a call, who should end the phone call first?   25.____
    A. The person who answered
    B. The person who called
    C. Either one – it doesn't matter
    D. A manager

KEY (CORRECT ANSWERS)

1. D
2. B
3. C
4. A
5. A

6. D
7. B
8. C
9. A
10. D

11. C
12. D
13. B
14. D
15. A

16. B
17. A
18. C
19. D
20. B

21. A
22. C
23. A
24. B
25. B

TEST 2

DIRECTIONS: Each question or incomplete statement is followed by several suggested answers or completions. Select the one that BEST answers the question or completes the statement. *PRINT THE LETTER OF THE CORRECT ANSWER IN THE SPACE AT THE RIGHT.*

1. Which of the following would be considered acceptable for an office clerk when answering the phone?
    A. Chewing gum
    B. Listening to music
    C. Eating a snack while on mute
    D. Wearing a headset

    1.____

2. Why would asking a caller for their phone number be important?
    A. In case they get disconnected
    B. To show them you are polite and considerate
    C. In case the caller is rude, this way you can call them back
    D. For future instances where calling residents back might make sense

    2.____

3. When rolling out a new program to help train employees in better customer service, the manager starts off by talking about the importance of telephone greetings.
    Why is this so important?
    A. It is the first impression the customer has of the department
    B. It shows the customer that employees are happy
    C. It shows that you are polite
    D. It isn't that important, but the manager thinks it is

    3.____

4. Which of the following is the MOST important aspect of an employee's voice in a telephone call?
    A. Their volume
    B. Their speed
    C. Their tone
    D. All of these aspects are equally important

    4.____

5. A clerk is on the phone with a customer when another customer walks into the building.
    If the clerk must put the caller on hold, what do they need to say or ask?
    A. "Would you like to be put on hold?"
    B. "I apologize for the inconvenience, but please hold."
    C. "Would it be OK if I put you on hold for a moment?"
    D. "I have to let you go. Please call back later."

    5.____

6. When a resident comes into your office for a face-to-face meeting, it is of increased importance that you communicate positively with your
    A. words
    B. body language
    C. tone
    D. none of the above

    6.____

7. A customer calls when employees are at an all-staff meeting. When calling the customer back, a clerk reaches their voicemail.
Which of the following information is the MOST important to leave?
   A. The date and time
   B. Ask them to call back
   C. The employee's telephone number
   D. Apologize repeatedly for missing their call

7.____

8. If an employee is in the middle of a conversation about town hall policy with a co-worker and the phone rings, what should the employee do?
   A. Get caller's information and call back after the conversation is finished
   B. Tell the co-worker to wait until finished with the phone call
   C. Answer the call and put caller on hold until conversation is finished
   D. Answer the call and transfer it to another employee who is not currently busy

8.____

9. When dealing with a resident who casually uses vulgar language, it is MOST appropriate for a town employee to
   A. tell the resident to come back when he learns how to speak
   B. converse with the resident using equally coarse language
   C. politely ask the resident to refrain from using vulgar language
   D. make the resident wait longer so he knows it won't be tolerated

9.____

10. The mayor's office has recently come under fire for a variety of perceived scandals.
In this emergency situation, which of the following would NOT be a recommended step in handling the crisis?
   A. Minimizing damage to the office's reputation through whatever means necessary
   B. Taking responsibility and apologizing
   C. Providing constant updates on the situation
   D. Designating one spokesperson to handle the relaying of updates

10.____

11. A resident complains that recreation center employees are using bureaucratic or overly technical communication. This type of language is often referred to as
   A. clichés   B. jargon   C. euphemisms   D. legalese

11.____

12. Which of the following strategies does an employee need to utilize to convince the public to believe a message that is contrary to their beliefs?
   A. Cognitive dissonance   B. Uses and gratification
   C. Sleeper effect   D. Source credibility

12.____

13. When communicating with parents of a summer camp run by the district, which of the following should NOT be a goal of the process?
   A. Motivation   B. Persuasion
   C. Mutual understanding   D. Isolation of the conflict

13.____

14. A manager comes up with a new procedure that he believes would improve the claims process that residents need to go through. Some employees agree that the procedure would make sense and others do not. One employee openly criticizes the idea to the manager.
Which of the following actions should the manager take?
He should
    A. meet with the employee for a talk and explain why bypassing his authority is unacceptable
    B. not respond to the critics in order to avoid unnecessary risks
    C. reprimand the employee who went over his head
    D. only implement the procedures that all agreed were good in order to satisfy employees

14.____

15. The county clerk's office is working on improving its employees' professionalism.
If employees are attempting to maintain a professional demeanor, what should they NOT do after making a mistake?
    A. Work to do better at the next opportunity
    B. Move on
    C. Accept responsibility
    D. Explain or rationalize the error

15.____

16. According to most recent surveys, data reveals that most white-collar workers
    A. have about a 25 percent efficiency rate when listening
    B. lose only about 25 percent efficiency when listening
    C. never take listening for granted
    D. learn to listen effectively since hearing is the important active learned process

16.____

17. Which of the following are NOT one of the four phases of listening to a customer?
    A. Hearing   B. Translating   C. Responding   D. Comprehending

17.____

18. Which of the following societal factors might impact a resident/employee interaction?
    A. Increased efficiency in technology
    B. Globalization of the economy
    C. More people between the ages of 16-24 entering the workplace
    D. Geopolitical changes

18.____

19. If a resident comes in confused about a policy change, which of the following approaches should an employee take to handle the situation?
    A. Communicate negatively when they need to
    B. Avoid gestures such as smiling or looking at customers when speaking to them
    C. Recognize how they tend to communicate and adjust accordingly if the customer is still showing signs of confusion
    D. Understand that many people are doubtful of good customer service

19.____

20. In order to avoid negative public perception, which of the following "finger pointing" words/phrases should be avoided when interacting with the public?
    A. Let me   B. You   C. Why   D. Yes

21. In an effort to improve government/resident relations, the mayor wants to roll out a new PR format that stresses public communication.
    Which of the following strategies should NOT be suggested as part of the PR campaign?
    A. Plan the message
    B. Greet residents warmly
    C. Listen carefully and respond appropriately
    D. Let the residents initiate conversations

22. A resident complains that the department does not always treat the local residents as people.
    Of the following, which would be the BEST strategy for resolving this issue?
    A. Accept responsibility and offer specific assistance
    B. Blame the customer when necessary
    C. Provide policies as reasons for actions
    D. None of the above

23. When providing feedback to residents, which of the following strategies is NOT effective?
    A. Remain emotional when providing feedback
    B. Confirm residents' meaning before offering feedback
    C. Ensure the feedback is appropriate to the original message
    D. Avoid extreme criticism or negative language

24. An employee at City Hall receives special treatment from his manager. This causes the employee to feel empowered, which then leads to him abusing authority and power.
    Which of the following would MOST likely happen if this behavior is allowed to continue?
    A. Other employees would begin to feel empowered
    B. Co-workers would work harder to demonstrate their commitment
    C. Residents would begin to work with the empowered employee because he would be able to get things done
    D. The rest of the department would start to feel resentment and frustration, and might potentially retaliate

25. If a town clerk works well with customers on the phone but struggles with face-to-face interactions, which of the following might BEST explain the problem?
    A. The actual words the clerk uses   B. Facial and other body cues
    C. Vocal cues   D. Both A and C

KEY (CORRECT ANSWERS)

1.	D		11.	B
2.	A		12.	A
3.	A		13.	D
4.	D		14.	A
5.	C		15.	D
6.	B		16.	A
7.	C		17.	B
8.	B		18.	C
9.	C		19.	C
10.	A		20.	B

21. D
22. A
23. A
24. D
25. B

TEST 3

DIRECTIONS: Each question or incomplete statement is followed by several suggested answers or completions. Select the one that BEST answers the question or completes the statement. *PRINT THE LETTER OF THE CORRECT ANSWER IN THE SPACE AT THE RIGHT.*

1. If an employee's body position is causing customers to feel she is projecting a mood/attitude that she isn't actually expressing, what does the employee need to work on improving?
   A. Pitch   B. Articulation   C. Posture   D. Inflection

1.____

2. A newly hired assistant notices that everyone in his department has received a new computer system except for him.
   What should he do?
   A. Assume this is a mistake and speak to his manager
   B. Complain to H.R.
   C. Quit
   D. Confront his manager regarding his unfair treatment

2.____

3. A team leader in your department notices that ample amounts of department-labeled property have come up missing in recent weeks. The leader notices a fellow supervisor putting stationery and other equipment into a personal bag on a few different occasions and believes this person is responsible.
   What is the LEAST effective response to the situation?
   A. Gather more evidence to catch the person in the act
   B. Do nothing – if guilty, someone else will likely catch the colleague
   C. Privately ask other colleagues if they've noticed anything suspicious recently
   D. Inform a supervisor higher up in the organization that this person is a potential suspect

3.____

4. Near the end of the work day, an official advisor accidentally sends an e-mail containing confidential information to the wrong person.
   Which of the following would be the BEST thing for the advisor to do?
   A. Overlook the error. Send the e-mail to the correct person and leave things as they are.
   B. Find a senior advisor and explain the mistake and have them deal with the problem
   C. Leave the office and deal with any fallout tomorrow
   D. Immediately send a follow-up e-mail to the "wrong" person explaining the mistake. Then send the e-mail to the correct person.

4.____

5. If an employee is engaged with a customer and no one else is around when the phone rings, what is the PROPER step to take in this situation?
   A. Let the phone ring and continue to work with the customer in person
   B. Take the call and address the caller's issue, then hang up and come back to the customer
   C. Ask the customer to answer the phone while trying to resolve their issue.
   D. Tell the customer "excuse me" while answering the phone, then put the caller on hold while going back to the customer

5.____

6. According to many national retailer surveys, what do consumers remember the MOST about their customer service experience?
   A. The cost of the merchandise/experience
   B. The demeanor of the employee who engaged them
   C. The cleanliness of the office/area
   D. How nice the employees were

6.____

7. When attempting to help a resident make a decision about programs offered by your agency, it is important to remember that the majority of purchasing decisions consumers make are based upon
   A. what they think   B. a potential free gift
   C. how they feel   D. all of the above

7.____

8. In an effort to improve procedures in your department, a memo has been sent to employees. In it, one highlighted section focuses on the importance of avoiding closed-ended questions/comments.
Following the advice of the memo, which question/comment should an employee avoid stating to a resident?
   A. "Can I help you?"
   B. "What is it you would like to see accomplished?"
   C. "So the challenges you've faced so far are..."
   D. "How would you like to see that improved?"

8.____

9. Numerous surveys indicate that consumers would actually pay more for
   A. self-checkout machines
   B. free product/demonstration giveaways
   C. more streamlined customer service
   D. apps using customer-service bots

9.____

10. Which of the following is an example of a proper "Activation Greeting"?
    A. "My name is _____. Let me tell you about our programs."
    B. "How many are there in your group?"
    C. "Hi! Welcome to _____."
    D. Both A and C

10.____

11. When interacting with members of the public, which of the following is the MOST important thing to do?
    A. Ask them to pay for services up front
    B. Smile at them
    C. Learn their name and call them by it
    D. Ask questions

11._____

12. Which of the following pieces of advice would help a clerk the MOST when working with the public?
    A. Pay attention to needs of others and offer only general solutions
    B. Hear what others are saying but do not take their comments to heart
    C. Focus on efficiency of service over quality of service
    D. Clearly understand the motives and needs of others

12._____

13. A member of the community complains that counselors at her child's camp do not listen to what she is telling them.
    Which technique listed below would improve understanding between the two parties?
    A. Reflective listening   B. Narrow selections
    C. Reflective thinking   D. Valid suggestions

13._____

14. When dealing with elderly residents, which of the following facts should be considered by a public official?
    A. They expect to be treated with courtesy and respect
    B. Expect them to avoid eye contact
    C. They prefer the telephone to personal contact
    D. They expect text and e-mail over face-to-face communication

14._____

15. If you are hired as a camp counselor for younger residents, it is important to remember all of the following about their behavior EXCEPT that they
    A. value technology
    B. are used to multitasking and access to instant information
    C. make less eye contact
    D. prefer more formal interactions

15._____

16. If one is trying to improve morale regarding customer/worker relations, which of the following is NOT a recommended thing to do?
    A. Publicly embarrass customers who are rude to the office employees
    B. Greet the customer with "Good Morning"
    C. Politely ask customers who cut in line to wait until it is their turn
    D. Thank customers for doing business with you

16._____

17. When hired by a public office, which of the following would be part of the newly hired employee's performance code?
    A. Report on time in a calm and controlled manner
    B. Present oneself in a neat and clean way
    C. Treat co-workers and residents with dignity and respect
    D. All of the above

17._____

18. If an employee sometimes "bends the rules" to honor a request from a customer, what service concept would explain this action?
    A. Motivated marketing strategy
    B. Power selling philosophy
    C. Employee empowerment
    D. Selling out for the customer

18.____

19. A Parks and Recreation worker is attempting to improve relations with the groups who sign up for his arts and crafts program.
    He should remember all of the following "Customer Service Rules" EXCEPT
    A. Customer service has a large effect on customer satisfaction
    B. Modern consumers are already more satisfied with customer service today than ever before
    C. Modern consumers have many different mechanisms by which to complain
    D. Feeling empowered as an employee usually leads to higher customer satisfaction

19.____

20. A marketing executive employee wishes to emphasize customer loyalty. Which of the following marketing strategies should the employee focus on when working with customers?
    A. Relationship marketing
    B. Undercover marketing
    C. Diversity marketing
    D. Transactional marketing

20.____

21. Why would a campaign manager for an elected official be interested in conducting a mail survey over other methods of surveying?
    It would
    A. avoid non-response problems
    B. speed up the process by which surveys are returned to them
    C. avoid participation by incorrect respondents
    D. enable the completion of the survey at a convenient time

21.____

22. At the end of each session, a counselor takes it upon herself to conduct research on the effectiveness of the program. She is worried that respondents won't be truthful, so she decides that the BEST way to avoid bias would be to conduct a(n) _____ survey.
    A. personal   B. telephone   C. internet   D. observational

22.____

23. A resident walks into the office and submits an application. When she is given additional forms to complete, she grumbles about "bureaucratic red tape" and how it's slowing down her application approval.
    How should an employee handle this situation?
    A. Be patient with the resident but do not explain the reason for the forms
    B. Tell the resident why the additional forms are necessary
    C. Suggest that the resident take it up with the manager if she wants the policy changed
    D. Say that the application will not be processed until ALL forms are completed

23.____

24. An employee's next-door neighbor has been hired as summer help, which the employee knows about because he has to type a confidential letter from the director to human resources about the hire. The neighbor does not yet know of the hiring decision, and the employee will see the neighbor later that day. Which one of the following should the employee do?
    A. Say nothing and wait for the offer to become official
    B. Congratulate the neighbor confidentially
    C. Inform a handful of people including the neighbor's close friends
    D. None of the above

25. A child with vision impairment wants to join a summer day camp and is denied access because the camp focuses on games and activities in which sight is required. If the parent comes in and complains to you, which of the following actions should you take and why?
    A. Modify the camp so the child can join because it is bad publicity to deny a child with a disability
    B. Offer another camp that does not focus on so many "sight-based" activities at a reduced rate so the parent and child do not feel left out
    C. Enroll the child and ensure they are allowed to participate in a meaningful way, because it's against the law to prevent the child from signing up
    D. Tell the parent they can talk to a supervisor because you have no authority to change the decision

KEY (CORRECT ANSWERS)

1.	C		11.	B
2.	A		12.	D
3.	B		13.	A
4.	D		14.	A
5.	D		15.	D
6.	B		16.	A
7.	C		17.	D
8.	A		18.	C
9.	C		19.	B
10.	C		20.	A

21. D
22. C
23. B
24. A
25. C

TEST 4

DIRECTIONS: Each question or incomplete statement is followed by several suggested answers or completions. Select the one that BEST answers the question or completes the statement. *PRINT THE LETTER OF THE CORRECT ANSWER IN THE SPACE AT THE RIGHT.*

1. If a customer tells an employee they need to work on having open body language, which of the following would be an example?
   A. Fiddling
   B. Minimal eye contact
   C. Folded arms
   D. Frequent hand gestures

   1.____

2. As a phone operator for the bureau director's office, it is important that you make the constituents feel as though you are actively listening to their concerns.
   What is the MOST effective way to demonstrate this?
   A. Use affirmation with words like "ok", "yes" and "I understand"
   B. Interrupt with your own thoughts
   C. Ask numerous closed questions
   D. Talk over the constituent

   2.____

3. When a resident walks up to a clerk's desk, which of the following is the BEST way to greet them?
   A. Wave
   B. Ask them what they need
   C. Welcome them and ask how they can be helped
   D. Ignore them until finished with the current task

   3.____

4. When a customer complains through e-mail, an office clerk should
   A. forward the e-mail to a supervisor
   B. reply right away with a potential solution
   C. share the complaint via the office's official Twitter handle
   D. reply right away with a hurried answer

   4.____

5. Interacting with the public is a constant back and forth where feedback is essential to improving service.
   Which of the following methods would be BEST to obtain feedback from the public?
   A. Cold calling
   B. Tweeting
   C. Survey via website
   D. Ask the staff what they think

   5.____

6. If residents continually complain that clerks do not truly understand what they are trying to tell them, which of the following practices might help improve this communication barrier?
   A. Paraphrasing
   B. Encoding
   C. Rapport building
   D. Decoding

   6.____

7. A customer complains to an employee and demands to see a supervisor. The employee is not sure to who to direct this angry customer. Which of the following methods of illustrating hierarchy of the company would help the employee out?
   A. Diagramming
   B. Negotiation
   C. Brainstorming
   D. Organizational charts

7.____

8. A village clerk and a resident have a strong disagreement about how an office policy applies to their situation. A co-worker is asked to weigh in on the situation. How should the co-worker handle the situation?
   A. Take the employee's side since they have to work side by side
   B. Try to help both parties walk away feeling like they got what they wanted
   C. Take the resident's side since the office cannot afford bad publicity
   D. Have a supervisor intervene – it's better to pass responsibility onto someone in power

8.____

9. A parent accuses your department of making generalizations about their child based on the group to which they belong. Which of the following unfair, but common, ideas is the department being accused of?
   A. Racism
   B. Stereotyping
   C. Confirmation bias
   D. Rationale judgment

9.____

10. When a resident calls a government office, they expect the phone to be picked up by the _____ ring otherwise they feel as though their call is unimportant.
    A. 1st
    B. 4th
    C. 3rd
    D. 7th

10.____

11. When working directly with a consumer on the phone or in person, which of the following would be considered inappropriate?
    A. Eating, drinking or chewing gum
    B. Speaking slowly and enunciating clearly
    C. Asking permission to put someone on hold
    D. Wearing a headset

11.____

12. Someone calls village hall and is extremely upset by a policy change enacted in the last board meeting. They demand an explanation that the clerk does not have.
    As the clerk tries to find the answer, how often should she update the angry caller on the status of the complaint (even if the clerk has no answer)?
    A. 2-3 minutes
    B. 35 seconds
    C. 1 minute
    D. Do not update them until an answer has been found

12.____

13. A resident is irate over how a co-worker of yours handled his claim process and now you have to handle his appeal. Throughout the process of filling out the necessary paperwork, this resident continues to not only berate the co-worker, but also starts complaining about how slow you are.
    In this stressful situation, why is it important to stay calm and not let the resident get to you?
    A. They could be having a bad day and your anger may make the situation worse
    B. You need to show the resident you are willing to take the time necessary to resolve his or her problem
    C. They might be violent and could end up hurting you
    D. Both A and B

14. An employee is calling residents to thank them for volunteering for a food drive. As the employee moves through his list, he accidentally dials the wrong number, and a person on the other line answers.
    What should the employee do?
    A. Apologize to the person for calling the wrong number
    B. Thank the person anyway
    C. Hang up before the person says anything else
    D. Try to sign the person up for the next food drive

15. Which of the following questions tell the customer that the employee wants to ensure that every need has been met before the interaction is over?
    A. "You've said everything you need to say, right?"
    B. "Is there anything else I can help you with?"
    C. "How can I help you today?"
    D. "Would you like me to transfer you to someone else?"

16. An elderly resident calls your department, but was trying to reach the Health and Sanitation Department. What should you do?
    A. Be polite
    B. Hastily transfer the person to the correct department
    C. Try to determine who they need to speak to and transfer them to that person directly if possible
    D. Both A and C

17. Which of the following would NOT be considered an example of good customer service?
    A. A parent waits three minutes to pick up their child from an after-school activity
    B. A clearly defined resolution process is in place for residents who have disagreements with public officials
    C. There is no line at the DMV, and a person waits 10 minutes before being serviced
    D. The park's pools briefly close at noon and 4 p.m. so they can be skimmed and checked for debris

18. A resident is angry about a zoning issue that prevents him from adding on to his garage.
When dealing with this customer, which of the following should an employee NOT do?
    A. Acknowledge their emotion
    B. Ask questions
    C. Avoid escalating the argument
    D. Agree that the code is silly

18.____

19. A resident comes into the office where you work and complains that he was screened out of a job because of a vision impairment. He asks if this is legal and what he should do.
You tell him it is not against the Americans With Disabilities Act if the employer screens him because
    A. clients prefer not to be served by the disabled
    B. a business cannot make a reasonable accommodation to work tasks for a specific disability
    C. co-workers dislike working with the disabled
    D. none of the above; ADA prevents any kind of "screening out" of disabled persons

19.____

20. During holidays and special events, the school office can sometimes be short-staffed, which requires all employees to know the different roles within the office. Some parents do not like when certain staff members act as the receptionist and those staff members do not like being the receptionist.
Since both sides do not like the employees in that role, the employees should
    A. learn the receptionist's job and fill in when needed, but tell the principal that they, and parents, would prefer that they work in a different area
    B. tell the principal they don't want to work as a receptionist and ask to be excused from that role
    C. learn the receptionist's job, but when asked to fill in ask someone else to do it
    D. ask the principal to excuse then from the training, and explain that other employees who the parents like more could fill in for them

20.____

21. In an attempt to promote the recreation center in a positive light, which of the following advertising strategies would be MOST credible to town residents?
    A. Employees telling people how great the recreation center environment is
    B. Have local celebrities endorse the recreation center as the place to be
    C. Use current satisfied customers by having them "spread the word" about the recreation center
    D. Offer incredible discounts to the first 25 new customers to sign up

21.____

22. When a clerk is tasked with setting up a Town Hall meeting, all of the following are important EXCEPT
    A. spreading the word
    B. having an audience-selected moderator
    C. setting and following a schedule
    D. keeping things moving

22.____

23. A librarian works in the computer lab and a patron comes to her and says, "My flash drive is full. I need to save the document I just created. Where can I get a new flash drive?"
How should the librarian respond?
    A. Offer to help the patron e-mail the document to himself and then show him how to do it
    B. Ask the patron what he needs to save and then save it to a "Google Document" for them
    C. Offer him the use of a library-owned flash drive on the promise that he will bring it back
    D. Direct him to the nearest computer/retail store to purchase the flash drive

24. If people call for a Town Hall meeting, which of the following would NOT be a good reason to hold one?
    A. To voice a common concern shared by members of the community
    B. To present a new proposal that impacts the public
    C. To settle a dispute between rival advisors at City Hall
    D. To collect feedback in response to a new rule or policy implementation

25. Of the following Town Hall meeting pitfalls, which would MOST leave residents feeling as though they wasted their time?
    A. Not participative or interactive
    B. Poorly designed PowerPoint or on-screen presentation
    C. Poor time management
    D. Meaningless or irrelevant content

KEY (CORRECT ANSWERS)

1.	D	11.	A
2.	A	12.	C
3.	C	13.	D
4.	B	14.	A
5.	C	15.	B
6.	A	16.	D
7.	D	17.	C
8.	B	18.	D
9.	B	19.	B
10.	C	20.	A

21. C
22. B
23. A
24. C
25. D

READING COMPREHENSION
UNDERSTANDING AND INTERPRETING WRITTEN MATERIAL
EXAMINATION SECTION
TEST 1

DIRECTIONS: Each question or incomplete statement is followed by several suggested answers or completions. Select the one that BEST answers the question or completes the statement. *PRINT THE LETTER OF THE CORRECT ANSWER IN THE SPACE AT THE RIGHT.*

Questions 1-8.

DIRECTIONS: Questions 1 through 8 are to be answered on the basis of the following regulations governing Newspaper Carriers when on subway trains or station platforms. These Newspaper Carriers are issued badges which entitle them to enter subway stations, when carrying papers in accordance with these regulations, without paying a fare.

REGULATIONS GOVERNING NEWSPAPER CARRIERS WHEN ON SUBWAY TRAINS OR STATION PLATFORMS

1. Carriers must wear badges at all times when on trains.
2. Carriers must not sort, separate, or wrap bundles on trains or insert sections.
3. Carriers must not obstruct platform of cars or stations.
4. Carriers may make delivery to stands inside the stations by depositing their badge with the station agent.
5. Throwing of bundles is strictly prohibited and will be cause for arrest.
6. Each bundle must not be over 18" x 12" x 15".
7. Not more than two bundles shall be carried by each carrier. (An extra fare to be charged for a second bundle.)
8. No wire to be used on bundles carried into stations.

1. These regulations do NOT prohibit carriers on trains from _____ newspapers.

   A. sorting bundles of
   B. carrying bundles of
   C. wrapping bundles of
   D. inserting sections into

2. A carrier delivering newspapers to a stand inside of the station MUST

   A. wear his badge at all times
   B. leave his badge with the railroad clerk
   C. show his badge to the railroad clerk
   D. show his badge at the newsstand

3. Carriers are warned against throwing bundles of newspapers from trains MAINLY because these acts may

   A. wreck the stand
   B. cause injury to passengers
   C. hurt the carrier
   D. damage the newspaper

4. It is permissible for a carrier to temporarily leave his bundles of newspapers 4.____

   A. near the subway car's door
   B. at the foot of the station stairs
   C. in front of the exit gate
   D. on a station bench

5. Of the following, the carrier who should NOT be restricted from entering the subway is 5.____
   the one carrying a bundle which is _____ long, _____ wide, and _____ high.

   A. 15"; 18"; 18" B. 18"; 12"; 18"
   C. 18"; 12"; 15" D. 18"; 15"; 15"

6. A carrier who will have to pay one fare is carrying _____ bundle(s). 6.____

   A. one   B. two   C. three   D. four

7. Wire may NOT be used for tying bundles because it may be 7.____

   A. rusty
   B. expensive
   C. needed for other purposes
   D. dangerous to other passengers

8. If a carrier is arrested in violation of these regulations, the PROBABLE reason is that he 8.____

   A. carried too many papers
   B. was not wearing his badge
   C. separated bundles of newspapers on the train
   D. tossed a bundle of newspapers to a carrier on a train

Questions 9-12.

DIRECTIONS: Questions 9 through 12 are to be answered on the basis of the Bulletin printed below. Read this Bulletin carefully before answering these questions. Select your answers ONLY on the basis of this Bulletin.

BULLETIN

Rule 107(m) states, in part, that *Before closing doors they (Conductors) must afford passengers an opportunity to detrain and entrain...*

Doors must be left open long enough to allow passengers to enter and exit from the train. Closing doors on passengers too quickly does not help to shorten the station stop and is a violation of the safety and courtesy which must be accorded to all our passengers.

The proper and effective way to keep passengers moving in and out of the train is to use the public address system. When the train is excessively crowded and passengers on the platform are pushing those in the cars, it may be necessary to close the doors after a reasonable period of time has been allowed.

Closing doors on passengers too quickly is a violation of rules and will be cause for disciplinary actions.

9. Which of the following statements is CORRECT about closing doors on passengers too quickly? It

   A. will shorten the running time from terminal to terminal
   B. shortens the station stop but is a violation of safety and courtesy
   C. does not help shorten the station stop time
   D. makes the passengers detrain and entrain quicker

10. The BEST way to get passengers to move in and out of cars quickly is to

    A. have the platform conductors urge passengers to move into doorways
    B. make announcements over the public address system
    C. start closing doors while passengers are getting on
    D. set a fixed time for stopping at each station

11. The conductor should leave doors open at each station stop long enough for passengers to

    A. squeeze into an excessively crowded train
    B. get from the local to the express train
    C. get off and get on the train
    D. hear the announcements over the public address system

12. Closing doors on passengers too quickly is a violation of rules and is cause for

    A. the conductor's immediate suspension
    B. the conductor to be sent back to the terminal for another assignment
    C. removal of the conductor at the next station
    D. disciplinary action to be taken against the conductor

Questions 13-15.

DIRECTIONS: Questions 13 through 15 are to be answered on the basis of the Bulletin printed below. Read this Bulletin carefully before answering these questions. Select your answers ONLY on the basis of this Bulletin.

BULLETIN

Conductors assigned to train service are not required to wear uniform caps from June 1 to September 30, inclusive.

Conductors assigned to platform duty are required to wear the uniform cap at all times. Conductors are reminded that they must furnish their badge numbers to anyone who requests same.

During the above-mentioned period, conductors may remove their uniform coats. The regulation summer short-sleeved shirts must be worn with the regulation uniform trousers. Suspenders are not permitted if the uniform coat is removed. Shoes are to be black but sandals, sneakers, suede, canvas, or two-tone footwear must not be worn.

Conductors may work without uniform tie if the uniform coat is removed. However, only the top collar button may be opened. The tie may not be removed if the uniform coat is worn.

13. Conductors assigned to platform duty are required to wear uniform caps

    A. at all times except from June 1 to September 30, inclusive
    B. whenever they are on duty
    C. only from June 1 to September 30, inclusive
    D. only when they remove their uniform coats

14. Suspenders are permitted ONLY if conductors wear

    A. summer short-sleeved shirts with uniform trousers
    B. uniform trousers without belt loops
    C. the type permitted by the authority
    D. uniform coats

15. A conductor MUST furnish his badge number to

    A. authority supervisors only
    B. members of special inspection only
    C. anyone who asks him for it
    D. passengers only

Questions 16-17.

DIRECTIONS: Questions 16 and 17 are to be answered SOLELY on the basis of the following Bulletin.

BULLETIN

Effective immediately, Conductors on trains equipped with public address systems shall make the following announcements in addition to their regular station announcement. At stations where passengers normally board trains from their homes or places of employment, the announcement shall be *Good Morning* or *Good Afternoon* or *Good Evening,* depending on the time of the day. At stations where passengers normally leave trains for their homes or places of employment, the announcement shall be *Have a Good Day* or *Good Night,* depending on the time of day or night.

16. The MAIN purpose of making the additional announcements mentioned in the Bulletin is MOST likely to

    A. keep passengers informed about the time of day
    B. determine whether the public address system works in case of an emergency
    C. make the passengers' ride more pleasant
    D. have the conductor get used to using the public address system

17. According to this Bulletin, a conductor should greet passengers boarding the *D* train at the Coney Island Station at 8 A.M. Monday by announcing

    A. Have a Good Day
    B. Good Morning
    C. Watch your step as you leave
    D. Good Evening

Questions 18-25.

DIRECTIONS: Questions 18 through 25 are to be answered on the basis of the information regarding the incident given below. Read this information carefully before answering these questions.

INCIDENT

As John Brown, a cleaner, was sweeping the subway station platform, in accordance with his assigned schedule, he was accused by Henry Adams of unnecessarily bumping him with the broom and scolded for doing this work when so many passengers were on the platform. Adams obtained Brown's badge number and stated that he would report the matter to the Transit Authority. Standing around and watching this were Mary Smith, a schoolteacher, Ann Jones, a student, and Joe Black, a maintainer, with Jim Roe, his helper, who had been working on one of the turnstiles. Brown thereupon proceeded to take the names and addresses of these people as required by the Transit Authority rule which directs that names and addresses of as many disinterested witnesses be taken as possible. Shortly thereafter, a train arrived at the station and Adams, as well as several other people, boarded the train and left. Brown went back to his work of sweeping the station.

18. The cleaner was sweeping the station at this time because

    A. the platform was unusually dirty
    B. there were very few passengers on the platform
    C. he had no regard for the passengers
    D. it was set by his work schedule

19. This incident proves that

    A. witnesses are needed in such cases
    B. porters are generally careless
    C. subway employees stick together
    D. brooms are dangerous in the subway

20. Joe Black was a

    A. helper   B. maintainer
    C. cleaner   D. teacher

21. The number of persons witnessing this incident was

    A. 2   B. 3   C. 4   D. 5

22. The addresses of witnesses are required so that they may later be

    A. depended on to testify   B. recognized
    C. paid   D. located

23. The person who said he would report this incident to the transit authority was

    A. Black   B. Adams   C. Brown   D. Roe

24. The ONLY person of the following who positively did NOT board the train was 24.____
    A. Brown   B. Smith   C. Adams   D. Jones

25. As a result of this incident, 25.____
    A. no action need be taken against the cleaner unless Adams makes a written complaint
    B. the cleaner should be given the rest of the day off
    C. the handles of the brooms used should be made shorter
    D. Brown's badge number should be changed

KEY (CORRECT ANSWERS)

1. B
2. B
3. B
4. D
5. C

6. A
7. D
8. D
9. C
10. B

11. C
12. D
13. B
14. D
15. C

16. C
17. B
18. D
19. A
20. B

21. C
22. D
23. B
24. A
25. A

TEST 2

DIRECTIONS: Each question or incomplete statement is followed by several suggested answers or completions. Select the one that BEST answers the question or completes the statement. *PRINT THE LETTER OF THE CORRECT ANSWER IN THE SPACE AT THE RIGHT.*

Questions 1-10.

DIRECTIONS: Questions 1 through 10 are to be answered on the basis of the information contained in the following safety rules. Read the rules carefully before answering these questions.

SAFETY RULES

Employees must take every precaution to prevent accidents, or injury to persons, or damage to property. For this reason, they must observe conditions of the equipment and tools with which they work, and the structures upon which they work.

It is the duty of all employees to report to their superior all dangerous conditions which they may observe. Employees must use every precaution to prevent the origin of fire. If they discover smoke or a fire in the subway, they shall proceed to the nearest telephone and notify the trainmaster giving their name, badge number, and location of the trouble.

In case of accidents on the subway system, employees must, if possible, secure the name, address, and telephone number of any passengers who may have been injured.

Employees at or near the location of trouble on the subway system, whether it be a fire or an accident, shall render all practical assistance which they are qualified to perform.

1. The BEST way for employees to prevent an accident is to

   A. secure the names of the injured persons
   B. arrive promptly at the location of the accident
   C. give their name and badge numbers to the trainmaster
   D. take all necessary precautions

2. In case of trouble, trackmen are NOT expected to

   A. report fires
   B. give help if they don't know how
   C. secure telephone numbers of persons injured in subway accidents
   D. give their badge number to anyone

3. Trackmen MUST

   A. be present at all fires
   B. see all accidents
   C. report dangerous conditions
   D. be the first to discover smoke in the subway

85

4. Observing conditions means to

   A. look at things carefully
   B. report what you see
   C. ignore things that are none of your business
   D. correct dangerous conditions

5. A dangerous condition existing on the subway system which a trackman should observe and report to his superior would be

   A. passengers crowding into trains
   B. trains running behind schedule
   C. tools in defective condition
   D. some newspapers on the track

6. If a trackman discovers a badly worn rail, he should

   A. not take any action
   B. remove the worn section of rail
   C. notify his superior
   D. replace the rail

7. The MAIN reason a trackman should observe the condition of his tools is

   A. so that they won't be stolen
   B. because they don't belong to him
   C. to prevent accidents
   D. because they cannot be replaced

8. If a passenger who paid his fare is injured in a subway accident, it is MOST important that an employee obtain the passenger's

   A. name
   B. age
   C. badge number
   D. destination

9. An employee who happens to be at the scene of an accident on a crowded station of the system should

   A. not give assistance unless he chooses to do so
   B. leave the scene immediately
   C. question all bystanders
   D. render whatever assistance he can

10. If a trackman discovers a fire at one end of a station platform and telephones the information to the trainmaster, he need NOT give

    A. the trainmaster's name
    B. the name of the station involved
    C. his own name
    D. the number of his badge

Questions 11-15.

DIRECTIONS: Questions 11 through 15 are to be answered on the basis of the information contained in the safety regulations given below. Refer to these rules in answering these questions.

REGULATIONS FOR SMALL GROUPS WHO MOVE FROM POINT TO POINT ON THE TRACKS

Employees who perform duties on the tracks in small groups and who move from point to point along the trainway must be on the alert at all times and prepared to clear the track when a train approaches without unnecessarily slowing it down. Underground at all times, and out-of-doors between sunset and sunrise, such employees must not enter upon the tracks unless each of them is equipped with an approved light. Flashlights must not be used for protection by such groups. Upon clearing the track to permit a train to pass, each member of the group must give a proceed signal, by hand or light, to the motorman of the train. Whenever such small groups are working in an area protected by caution lights or flags, but are not members of the gang for whom the flagging protection was established, they must not give proceed signals to motormen. The purpose of this rule is to avoid a motorman's confusing such signal with that of the flagman who is protecting a gang. Whenever a small group is engaged in work of an engrossing nature or at any time when the view of approaching trains is limited by reason of curves or otherwise, one man of the group, equipped with a whistle, must be assigned properly to warn and protect the man or men at work and must not perform any other duties while so assigned.

11. If a small group of men are traveling along the tracks toward their work location and a train approaches, they should

    A. stop the train
    B. signal the motorman to go slowly
    C. clear the track
    D. stop immediately

11._____

12. Small groups may enter upon the tracks

    A. only between sunset and sunrise
    B. provided each has an approved light
    C. provided their foreman has a good flashlight
    D. provided each man has an approved flashlight

12._____

13. After a small group has cleared the tracks in an area unprotected by caution lights or flags,

    A. each member must give the proceed signal to the motorman
    B. the foreman signals the motorman to proceed
    C. the motorman can proceed provided he goes slowly
    D. the last member off the tracks gives the signal to the motorman

13._____

14. If a small group is working in an area protected by the signals of a track gang, the members of the small group

    A. need not be concerned with train movement
    B. must give the proceed signal together with the track gang

14._____

      C. can delegate one of their members to give the proceed signal
      D. must not give the proceed signal

15. If the view of approaching trains is blocked, the small group should

      A. move to where they can see the trains
      B. delegate one of the group to warn and protect them
      C. keep their ears alert for approaching trains
      D. refuse to work at such locations

Questions 16-25.

DIRECTIONS: Questions 16 through 25 are to be answered SOLELY on the basis of the article about general safety precautions given below.

GENERAL SAFETY PRECAUTIONS

When work is being done on or next to a track on which regular trains are running, special signals must be displayed as called for in the general rules for flagging. Yellow caution signals, green clear signals, and a flagman with a red danger signal are required for the protection of traffic and workmen in accordance with the standard flagging rules. The flagman shall also carry a white signal for display to the motorman when he may proceed. The foreman in charge must see that proper signals are displayed.

On elevated lines during daylight hours, the yellow signal shall be a yellow flag, the red signal shall be a red flag, the green signal shall be a green flag, and the white signal shall be a white flag. In subway sections, and on elevated lines after dark, the yellow signal shall be a yellow lantern, the red signal shall be a red lantern, the green signal shall be a green lantern, and the white signal shall be a white lantern.

Caution and clear signals are to be secured to the elevated or subway structure with non-metallic fastenings outside the clearance line of the train and on the motorman's side of the track.

16. On elevated lines during daylight hours, the caution signal is a

      A. yellow lantern   B. green lantern
      C. yellow flag   D. green flag

17. In subway sections, the clear signal is a

      A. yellow lantern   B. green lantern
      C. yellow flag   D. green flag

18. The MINIMUM number of lanterns that a subway track flagman should carry is

      A. 1   B. 2   C. 3   D. 4

19. The PRIMARY purpose of flagging is to protect the

      A. flagman   B. motorman
      C. track workers   D. railroad

20. A suitable fastening for securing caution lights to the elevated or subway structure is

    A. copper nails
    B. steel wire
    C. brass rods
    D. cotton twine

21. On elevated structures during daylight hours, the red flag is held by the

    A. motorman   B. foreman   C. trackman   D. flagman

22. The signal used in the subway to notify a motorman to proceed is a

    A. white lantern
    B. green lantern
    C. red flag
    D. yellow flag

23. The caution, clear, and danger signals are displayed for the information of

    A. trackmen   B. workmen   C. flagmen   D. motormen

24. Since the motorman's cab is on the right-hand side, caution signals should be secured to the

    A. right-hand running rail
    B. left-hand running rail
    C. structure to the right of the track
    D. structure to the left of the track

25. In a track work gang, the person responsible for the proper display of signals is the

    A. track worker
    B. foreman
    C. motorman
    D. flagman

KEY (CORRECT ANSWERS)

1.	D	11.	C
2.	B	12.	B
3.	C	13.	A
4.	A	14.	D
5.	C	15.	B
6.	C	16.	C
7.	C	17.	B
8.	A	18.	B
9.	D	19.	C
10.	A	20.	D
21.	D		
22.	A		
23.	D		
24.	C		
25.	B		

TEST 3

DIRECTIONS: Each question or incomplete statement is followed by several suggested answers or completions. Select the one that BEST answers the question or completes the statement. *PRINT THE LETTER OF THE CORRECT ANSWER IN THE SPACE AT THE RIGHT.*

Questions 1-6.

DIRECTIONS: Questions 1 through 6 are to be answered on the basis of the Bulletin Order given below. Refer to this bulletin when answering these questions.

BULLETIN ORDER NO. 67

SUBJECT: Procedure for Handling Fire Occurrences

In order that the Fire Department may be notified of all fires, even those that have been extinguished by our own employees, any employee having knowledge of a fire must notify the Station Department Office immediately on telephone extensions D-4177, D-4181, D-4185, or D-4189.

Specific information regarding the fire should include the location of the fire, the approximate distance north or south of the nearest station, and the track designation, line, and division.

In addition, the report should contain information as to the status of the fire and whether our forces have extinguished it or if Fire Department equipment is required.

When all information has been obtained, the Station Supervisor in Charge in the Station Department Office will notify the Desk Trainmaster of the Division involved.

Richard Roe,
Superintendent

1. An employee having knowledge of a fire should FIRST notify the

   A. Station Department Office
   B. Fire Department
   C. Desk Trainmaster
   D. Station Supervisor

2. If bulletin order number 1 was issued on January 2, bulletins are being issued at the monthly average of

   A. 8   B. 10   C. 12   D. 14

3. It is clear from the bulletin that

   A. employees are expected to be expert fire fighters
   B. many fires occur on the transit system
   C. train service is usually suspended whenever a fire occurs
   D. some fires are extinguished without the help of the Fire Department

4. From the information furnished in this bulletin, it can be assumed that the

   A. Station Department office handles a considerable number of telephone calls
   B. Superintendent Investigates the handling of all subway fires
   C. Fire Department is notified only in ease of large fires
   D. employee first having knowledge of the fire must call all 4 extensions

5. The PROBABLE reason for notifying the Fire Department even when the fire has been extinguished by a subway employee is because the Fire Department is

   A. a city agency
   B. still responsible to check the fire
   C. concerned with fire prevention
   D. required to clean up after the fire

6. Information about the fire NOT specifically required is

   A. track   B. time of day   C. station   D. division

Questions 7-10.

DIRECTIONS: Questions 7 through 10 are to be answered on the basis of the paragraph on fire fighting shown below. When answering these questions, refer to this paragraph.

FIRE FIGHTING

A security officer should remember the cardinal rule that water or soda acid fire extinguishers should not be used on any electrical fire, and apply it in the case of a fire near the third rail. In addition, security officers should familiarize themselves with all available fire alarms and fire-fighting equipment within their assigned posts. Use of the fire alarm should bring responding Fire Department apparatus quickly to the scene. Familiarity with the fire-fighting equipment near his post would help in putting out incipient fires. Any man calling for the Fire Department should remain outside so that he can direct the Fire Department to the fire. As soon as possible thereafter, the special inspection desk must be notified, and a complete written report of the fire, no matter how small, must be submitted to this office. The security officer must give the exact time and place it started, who discovered it, how it was extinguished, the damage done, cause of same, list of any injured persons with the extent of their injuries, and the name of the Fire Chief in charge. All defects noticed by the security officer concerning the fire alarm or any fire-fighting equipment must be reported to the special inspection department.

7. It would be PROPER to use water to put out a fire in a(n)

   A. electric motor   B. electric switch box
   C. waste paper trash can   D. electric generator

8. After calling the Fire Department from a street box to report a fire, the security officer should then

   A. return to the fire and help put it out
   B. stay outside and direct the Fire Department to the fire
   C. find a phone and call his boss
   D. write out a report for the special inspection desk

9. A security officer is required to submit a complete written report of a fire

   A. two weeks after the fire
   B. the day following the fire
   C. as soon as possible
   D. at his convenience

10. In his report of a fire, it is NOT necessary for the security officer to state

    A. time and place of the fire
    B. who discovered the fire
    C. the names of persons injured
    D. quantity of Fire Department equipment used

Questions 11-16.

DIRECTIONS: Questions 11 through 16 are to be answered on the basis of the Notice given below. Refer to this Notice in answering these questions.

NOTICE

Your attention is called to Route Request Buttons that are installed on all new type Interlocking Home Signals where there is a choice of route in the midtown area. The route request button is to be operated by the motorman when the home signal is at danger and no call-on is displayed or when improper route is displayed.

To operate, the motorman will press the button for the desiredroute as indicated under each button; a light will then go on over the buttons to inform the motorman that his request has been registered in the tower.

If the towerman desires to give the motorman a route other than the one he selected, the towerman will cancel out the light over the route selection buttons. The motorman will then accept the route given.

If no route or call-on is given, the motorman will sound his whistle for the signal maintainer, secure his train, and call the desk trainmaster.

11. The official titles of the two classes of employee whose actions would MOST frequently be affected by the contents of this notice are

    A. motorman and trainmaster
    B. signal maintainer and trainmaster
    C. towerman and motorman
    D. signal maintainer and towerman

12. A motorman should use a route request button when

    A. the signal indicates proceed on main line
    B. a call-on is displayed
    C. the signal indicates stop
    D. the signal indicates proceed on diverging route

13. The PROPER way to request a route is to 13.____

    A. press the button corresponding to the desired route
    B. press the button a number of times to correspond with the number of the route requested
    C. stop at the signal and blow four short blasts
    D. stop at the signal and telephone the tower

14. The motorman will know that his requested route has been registered in the tower if 14.____

    A. a light comes on over the route request buttons
    B. an acknowledging signal is sounded on the tower horn
    C. the light in the route request button goes dark
    D. the home signal continues to indicate stop

15. Under certain conditions, when stopped at such home signal, the motorman must signal for a signal maintainer and call the desk trainmaster. 15.____
    Such condition exists when, after standing awhile,

    A. the towerman continues to give the wrong route
    B. the towerman does not acknowledge the signal
    C. no route or call-on is given
    D. the light over the route request buttons is cancelled out

16. It is clear that route request buttons 16.____

    A. eliminate train delays due to signals at junctions
    B. keep the towerman alert
    C. force motormen and towermen to be more careful
    D. are a more accurate form of communication than the whistle.

Questions 17-22.

DIRECTIONS: Questions 17 through 22 are to be answered on the basis of the instructions for removal of paper given below. Read these instructions carefully before answering these questions.

GENERAL INSTRUCTIONS FOR REMOVAL OF PAPER

When a cleaner's work schedule calls for the bagging of paper, he will remove paper from the waste paper receptacles, bag it, and place the bags at the head end of the platform, where they will be picked up by the work train. He will fill bags with paper to a weight that can be carried without danger of personal injury, as porters are forbidden to drag bags of paper over the platform. Cleaners are responsible that all bags of paper are arranged so as to prevent their falling from the platform to tracks, and so as to not interfere with passenger traffic.

17. A GOOD reason for removing the paper from receptacles and placing it in bags is that bags are more easily 17.____

    A. stored   B. weighed   C. handled   D. emptied

18. The *head end* of a local station platform is the end 18._____

    A. in the direction that trains are running
    B. nearest to which the trains stop
    C. where there is an underpass to the other side
    D. at which the change booth is located

19. The MOST likely reason for having the filled bags placed at the head end of the station rather than at the other end is that 19._____

    A. a special storage space is provided there for them
    B. this end of the platform is farthest from the passengers
    C. most porters' closets are located near the head end
    D. the work train stops at this end to pick them up

20. Limiting the weight to which the bags can be filled is PROBABLY done to 20._____

    A. avoid having too many ripped or broken bags
    B. protect the porter against possible rupture
    C. make sure that all bags are filled fairly evenly
    D. insure that, when stored, the bags will not fall to the track

21. The MOST important reason for not allowing filled bags to be dragged over the platform is that the bags 21._____

    A. could otherwise be loaded too heavily
    B. might leave streaks on the platform
    C. would wear out too quickly
    D. might spill paper on the platform

22. The instructions do NOT hold a porter responsible for a bag of paper which 22._____

    A. is torn due to dragging over a platform
    B. falls on a passenger because it was poorly stacked
    C. falls to the track without being pushed
    D. is ripped open by school children

Questions 23-25.

DIRECTIONS: Questions 23 through 25 are to be answered on the basis of the situation described below. Consider the facts given in this situation when answering these questions.

SITUATION

A new detergent that is to be added to water and the resulting mixture just wiped on any surface has been tested by the station department and appeared to be excellent. However, you notice, after inspecting a large number of stations that your porters have cleaned with this detergent, that the surfaces cleaned are not as clean as they formerly were when the old method was used.

23. The MAIN reason for the station department testing the new detergent in the first place was to make certain that

    A. it was very simple to use
    B. a little bit would go a long way
    C. there was no stronger detergent on the market
    D. it was superior to anything formerly used

24. The MAIN reason that such a poor cleaning job resulted was MOST likely due to the

    A. porters being lax on the job
    B. detergent not being as good as expected
    C. incorrect amount of water being mixed with the detergent
    D. fact that the surfaces cleaned needed to be scrubbed

25. The reason for inspecting a number of stations was to

    A. determine whether all porters did the same job
    B. insure that the result of the cleaning job was the same in each location
    C. be certain that the detergent was used in each station inspected
    D. see whether certain surfaces cleaned better than others

23. ____
24. ____
25. ____

KEY (CORRECT ANSWERS)

1.	A	11.	C
2.	C	12.	C
3.	D	13.	A
4.	A	14.	A
5.	C	15.	C
6.	B	16.	D
7.	C	17.	C
8.	B	18.	A
9.	C	19.	D
10.	D	20.	B

21. C
22. D
23. D
24. B
25. B

READING COMPREHENSION
UNDERSTANDING AND INTERPRETING WRITTEN MATERIAL

EXAMINATION SECTION

DIRECTIONS: Each question or incomplete statement is followed by several suggested answers or completions. Select the one that BEST answers the question or completes the statement. *PRINT THE LETTER OF THE CORRECT ANSWER IN THE SPACE AT THE RIGHT.*

TEST 1

Questions 1-2.

DIRECTIONS: Questions 1 and 2 are to be answered SOLELY on the basis of the following passage.

One of the biggest mistakes of government executives with substantial supervisory responsibility is failing to make careful appraisals of performance during employee probationary periods. Many a later headache could have been avoided by prompt and full appraisal during the early months of an employee's assignment. There is not much more to say about this except to emphasize the common prevalence of this oversight and to underscore that for its consequences, which are many and sad, the offending managers have no one to blame but themselves.

1. According to the above passage, probationary periods are
    A. a mistake and should not be used by supervisors with large responsibilities
    B. not used properly by government executives
    C. used only for those with supervisory responsibility
    D. the consequence of management mistakes

2. The one of the following conclusions that can MOST appropriately be drawn from the above passage is that
    A. management's failure to appraise employees during their probationary period is a common occurrence
    B. there is not much to say about probationary periods because they are unimportant
    C. managers should blame employees for failing to use their probationary periods properly
    D. probationary periods are a headache to most managers

Questions 3-7.

DIRECTIONS: Questions 3 through 7 are to be answered SOLELY on the basis of the passage preceding each question.

97

3. Things may not always be what they seem to be. Thus, the wise supervisor should analyze his problems and determine whether there is something there that does not meet the eye. For example, what may seem on the surface to be a personality clash between two subordinates may really be a problem of faulty organization, bad communication, or bad scheduling.
Which one of the following statements BEST supports this passage?
   A. The wise supervisor should avoid personality clashes.
   B. The smart supervisor should figure out what really is going on.
   C. Bad scheduling is the result of faulty organization.
   D. The best supervisor is the one who communicates effectively.

4. Some supervisors, under the pressure of meeting deadlines, become harsh and dictatorial to their subordinates. However, the supervisor most likely to be effective in meeting deadlines is one who absorbs or cushions pressures from above. According to the above passage, if a supervisor wishes to meet deadlines, it is MOST important that he
   A. be informative to his superiors
   B. encourage personal initiative among his subordinates
   C. become harsh and dictatorial to his subordinates
   D. protects his subordinates from pressures from above

5. When giving instructions, a supervisor must always make clear his meaning, leaving no room for misunderstanding. For example, a supervisor who tells a subordinate to do a task *as soon as possible* might legitimately be understood to mean either *it's top priority* or *do it when you can*. Which of the following statements is BEST supported by the above passage?
   A. Subordinates will attempt to avoid work by deliberately distorting instructions.
   B. Instructions should be short, since brief instructions are the clearest.
   C. Less educated subordinates are more likely to honestly misunderstand instructions.
   D. A supervisor should give precise instructions that cannot be misinterpreted.

6. Practical formulas are often suggested to simplify what a supervisor should know and how he should behave, such as the four F's (be firm, fair, friendly, and factual). But such simple formulas are really broad principles, not necessarily specific guides in a real situation. According to the above passage, simple formulas for supervisory behavior
   A. are superior to complicated theories and principles
   B. not always of practical use in actual situations
   C. useful only if they are fair and factual
   D. would be better understood if written in clear language

7. Many management decisions are made far removed from the actual place of operations. Therefore, there is a great need for reliable reports and records and, the larger the organization, the greater is the need for such reports and records. According to the above passage, management decisions made far from the place of operations are
   A. dependent to a great extent on reliable reports and records
   B. sometimes in error because of the great distances involved
   C. generally unreliable because of poor communications
   D. generally more accurate than on-the-scene decisions

Questions 8-9.

DIRECTIONS: Questions 8 and 9 are to be answered SOLELY on the basis of the following passage.

A supervisor who is seeking to influence the behavior of others, whether these others are subordinates, superiors, or colleagues, soon becomes aware of the importance of their attitudes. He may be surprised at some of the attitudes they have and wonder how they can hold some of the views they do - if these views differ from his own. He may be perplexed when others do not change their attitudes even after he has presented facts that obviously should cause them to change.

8. Of the following, the MAIN implication of the above passage is that
    A. behavior is influenced by factual data
    B. interaction with others is based on factual data
    C. rank and intelligence determine behavior
    D. interpretation of facts is controlled by attitude

9. The one of the following statements MOST directly supported by the above paragraph is:
    A. A competent supervisor is firm in his views yet retains an open mind
    B. Influencing the behavior of others is usually the most difficult problem in effective supervision
    C. A particular viewpoint may seem unusual to a supervisor holding a contrary opinion
    D. Organizational success depends upon supervisory motivation

Questions 10-13.

DIRECTIONS: Questions 10 through 13 are to be answered SOLELY on the basis of the following passage.

Top public officials, who feel they have tried to improve conditions for their employees, are often bewildered, hurt, or angered when these employees want to do something on their own through union membership. These officials gain little, however, by regarding unionization as an insult or as evidence of failure on their part. The real challenge and opportunity for top officials is to deal constructively with the labor organization which their employees have *duly* chosen to represent them.

10. The author of the above passage MOST likely considers top management to be
    A. corrupt   B. independent
    C. entrenched   D. paternalistic

11. The above passage points out that certain top public officials are LIKELY to be
    A. disturbed that employees wish to be unionized
    B. aware of the actual needs of their employees
    C. convinced that labor organizations are ineffectual in gaining benefits
    D. unable to deal constructively with individual employees

12. The tenor of the above passage suggests that
    A. top officials should deal positively with the labor organization
    B. intelligent management practices usually eliminate labor union activities
    C. the labor movement has often opposed enlightened management policies
    D. labor and management have had a long history of disagreement

13. As used in the above passage, the word *duly* means MOST NEARLY
    A. properly or legally   B. forcefully or sincerely
    C. openly or publicly   D. precisely or carefully

Questions 14-17.

DIRECTIONS: Questions 14 through 17 are to be answered SOLELY on the basis of the following passage.

The mental attitude of the employee toward safety is exceedingly important in preventing accidents. All efforts designed to keep safety on the employee's mind and to keep accident prevention a live subject in the office will help substantially in a safety program. Although it may seem strange, it is common for people to be careless. Therefore, safety education is a continuous process.

Safety rules should be explained, and the reasons for their rigid enforcement should be given to employees. Telling employees to be careful or giving similar general safety warnings and slogans is probably of little value. Employees should be informed of basic safety fundamentals. This can be done through staff meetings, informal suggestions to employees, movies, and safety instruction cards. Safety instruction cards provide the employees with specific suggestions about safety and serve as a series of timely reminders helping to keep safety on the minds of employees. Pictures, posters, and cartoon sketches on bulletin boards that are located in areas continually used by employees arouse the employees' interest in safety. It is usually good to supplement this type of safety promotion with intensive individual follow-up.

14. The above passage implies that the LEAST effective of the following safety measures is
    A. rigid enforcement of safety rules
    B. getting employees to think in terms of safety
    C. elimination of unsafe conditions in the office
    D. telling employees to stay alert at all times

15. The reason given by the above passage for maintaining ongoing safety education is that
    A. people are often careless
    B. office tasks are often dangerous
    C. the value of safety slogans increases with repetition
    D. safety rules change frequently

16. Which one of the following safety aids is MOST likely to be preferred by the above passage? 16._____
    A
    A. cartoon of a man tripping over a carton and yelling, *Keep aisles clear!*
    B. poster with a large number one and a caption saying, *Safety First*
    C. photograph of a very neatly arranged office
    D. large sign with the word *THINK* in capital letters

17. Of the following, the BEST title for the above passage is 17._____
    A. BASIC SAFETY FUNDAMENTALS
    B. ENFORCING SAFETY AMONG CARELESS EMPLOYEES
    C. ATTITUDES TOWARD SAFETY
    D. MAKING EMPLOYEES AWARE OF SAFETY

Questions 18-21.

DIRECTIONS: Questions 18 through 21 are to be answered SOLELY on the basis of the following passage.

An employee who has been a member of the retirement system continuously for at least two years may thereafter borrow an amount not exceeding forty percent of the amount of his accumulated contributions in the retirement system, provided that he can repay the amount borrowed, with interest, before he reaches age sixty-three by additional deductions of eight percent from his compensation at the time it is paid. The rate of interest payable on such loan shall be three percent higher than the rate of regular interest creditable to his retirement account. The amount borrowed, with interest, shall be repaid in equal installments by deduction from the member's compensation at the time it is paid, but such installments must be equal to at least four percent of the member's compensation.

Each loan shall be insured by the retirement system against the death of the member, as follows: from the twenty-fifth through the fiftieth day after making the loan, thirty percent of the present value of the loan is insured; from the fifty-first through the seventy-fifth day, sixty percent of the present value of the loan is insured; on and after the seventy-sixth day, all of the present value of the loan is insured. Upon the death of the member, the amount of insurance payable shall be credited to his accumulated contributions to the retirement system.

Instead of a loan, any member who cancels his rate of contribution may withdraw from his account, and may restore in any year he chooses, any sum in excess of the maximum in his annuity savings account and due to his account at the end of the calendar year in which he was entitled to cancel his rate of contribution.

18. Based on the information in the above passage, a member may obtain a loan 18._____
    A. in any amount not exceeding forty percent of his accumulated contributions in the system
    B. if he has contributions in excess of the maximum in his annuity savings account
    C. if he will remain a member of the retirement system until age 63
    D. once during his first two years of membership and then at any time thereafter

19. According to the information in the above passage, the interest rate paid by a member who borrows from the retirement system is
    A. 4% of his earnable compensation
    B. 8% of his earnable compensation
    C. lower than the interest rate creditable to his retirement account
    D. higher than the interest rate creditable to his retirement account

20. Suppose that a member of the retirement system obtained a loan on July 15 of this year and died on October 2 when the present value of her loan was $800. Based on the information in the above passage, this member will have _____ her accumulated contributions to the retirement system.
    A. $480 credited to   B. $480 deducted from
    C. $800 credited to   D. $800 deducted from

21. Based on the information in the above passage, a member who has excess funds in his retirement account may with- draw funds from the retirement system
    A. if he has cancelled his rate of contribution
    B. if he restores the funds within one year of withdrawal
    C. when he retires
    D. if he leaves city service

Questions 22-25.

DIRECTIONS: Questions 22 through 25 are to be answered SOLELY on the basis of the following passage.

Upon the death of a member or former member of the retirement system, there shall be paid to his estate, or to the person he had nominated by written designation, his accumulated deductions. In addition, if he is a member who is in city service, there shall be paid a sum consisting of: an amount equal to the compensation he earned while a member during the three months immediately preceding his death, or, if the total amount of years of allowable service exceeds five, there shall be paid an amount equal to the compensation he earned while a member during the six months immediately preceding his death; and the reserve-for-increased-take-home-pay, if any. Payment for the expense of burial, not exceeding two hundred and fifty dollars, may be made to the relative or friend who, in the absence or failure of the designated beneficiary, assumes this responsibility.

Until the first retirement benefit payment has been made, where a member has not selected an option, the member will be considered to be in city service, and the death benefits provided above will be paid instead of the retirement allowance. The member, or upon his death his designated beneficiary, may provide that the actuarial equivalent of the benefit otherwise payable in a lump sum shall be paid in the form of an annuity payable in installments; the amount of such annuity is determined at the time of the member's death on the basis of the age of the beneficiary at that time.

22. Suppose that a member who has applied for retirement benefits without selecting an option dies before receiving any payments.
    According to the information in the above passage, this member's beneficiary would be entitled to receive
    A. an annuity based on the member's age at the time of his death
    B. a death benefit only
    C. the member's retirement allowance only
    D. the member's retirement allowance, plus a death benefit payment in a lump sum

22._____

23. According to the information in the above passage, the amount of the benefit payable upon the death of a member is based, in part, on the
    A. length of city service during which the deceased person was a member
    B. number of beneficiaries the deceased member had nominated
    C. percent of the deceased member's deductions for social security
    D. type of retirement plan to which the deceased member belonged

23._____

24. According to the information in the above passage, which one of the following statements concerning the payment of death benefits is CORRECT?
    A. In order for a death benefit to be paid, the deceased member must have previously nominated, in writing, someone to receive the benefit.
    B. Death benefits are paid upon the death of members who are in city service.
    C. A death benefit must be paid in one lump sum.
    D. When a retired person dies, his retirement allowance is replaced by a death benefit payment.

24._____

25. According to the information in the above passage, the amount of annuity payments made to a beneficiary in monthly installments in lieu of a lump sum payment is determined by the
    A. length of member's service at the time of his death
    B. age of the beneficiary at the time of the member's death
    C. member's age at retirement
    D. member's age at the time of his death

25._____

KEY (CORRECT ANSWERS)

1.	B	11.	A	21.	A
2.	A	12.	A	22.	B
3.	B	13.	A	23.	A
4.	D	14.	D	24.	B
5.	D	15.	A	25.	B
6.	B	16.	A		
7.	A	17.	D		
8.	D	18.	A		
9.	C	19.	D		
10.	D	20.	C		

TEST 2

DIRECTIONS: Each question or incomplete statement is followed by several suggested answers or completions. Select the one that BEST answers the question or completes the statement. *PRINT THE LETTER OF THE CORRECT ANSWER IN THE SPACE AT THE RIGHT.*

Questions 1-4.

DIRECTIONS: Questions 1 through 4 are to be answered SOLELY on the basis of the following passage.

Depreciation -- Any reduction from the upper limit of value. An effect caused by deterioration and/or obsolescence. Deterioration is evidenced by wear and tear, decay, dry rot, cracks, encrustations, or structural defects. Obsolescence is divisible into two parts, functional or economic. Functional obsolescence may be due to poor planning, mechanical inadequacy or overadequacy, functional inadequacy or overadequacy due to size, style, or age. It is evidenced by conditions within the property. Economic obsolescence is caused by changes external to the property, such as neighborhood infiltrations of inharmonious groups or property uses, legislation, etc. It is also the actual decline in market value of the improvement to land from the time of purchase to the time of sale.

1. According to the above passage, a form of physical deterioration can be caused by
    A. termite infestation
    B. zoning regulations
    C. inadequate wiring
    D. extra high ceilings

2. According to the above passage, a form of economic obsolescence may be caused by
    A. structural defects
    B. poor architectural design
    C. changes in zoning regulations
    D. chemical reactions

3. According to the above passage, the statement which BEST explains the meaning of depreciation is that it is a loss in value
    A. caused only by economic obsolescence
    B. resulting from any cause
    C. caused only by wear and tear
    D. resulting from conditions or changes external to the property

4. According to the above passage, the lack of air conditioning in warm climates is
    A. a form of physical deterioration
    B. a form of functional obsolescence
    C. a form of economic obsolescence
    D. not a form of depreciation

Questions 5-8.

DIRECTIONS: Questions 5 through 8 are to be answered SOLELY on the basis of the following passage.

In determining the valuation of income-producing property, the capitalization of income is accepted as a proper approach to value. Income-producing property is bought and sold for the purpose of making money. How much an investor would pay would, of course, depend on how much he could earn on his investment. The amount he would earn on his investment is called a return. The amount of return depends on the degree of risk involved.

If one has $100,000 to invest, it can be put in a bank account at perhaps a 5 percent return. In the bank, the money is relatively safe so the return is lower. If the money were invested by purchasing a block of stores in a depressed area, of course, one would not be satisfied with a 5 percent return. This is what the capitalization of income comes down to - the better the return, the higher the risk. This is the approach an experienced real estate investor uses in determining what he would pay for property.

5. According to the above passage, which one of the following investments would an experienced real estate investor with $100,000 MOST likely choose? A(n)
   A. apartment building in a slum area yielding a 6 percent return
   B. office building rented to professionals yielding a 6 percent return
   C. shopping center in a depressed area yielding a 10 percent return
   D. warehouse rented on a long-term lease to a major corporation yielding a 10 percent return

5._____

6. According to the above passage, in the capitalization of income, the relationship between the degree of risk and the rate of return GENERALLY is expected to be
   A. indeterminate   B. variable
   C. inverse   D. direct

6._____

7. According to the above passage, in purchasing income-producing property, the one of the following which would NOT be a factor influencing an experienced real estate investor is the
   A. socio-economic characteristics of the area in which the property is located
   B. rate of return on investment
   C. original cost of the property
   D. degree of risk involved

7._____

8. According to the above passage, the property listed below which would be LEAST likely to be valued by the capitalization of income is a(n)
   A. apartment house with no vacancies
   B. office building rented to 70 percent of capacity
   C. shopping center with several new tenants
   D. vacant lot located next to a factory

8._____

Questions 9-12.

DIRECTIONS: Questions 9 through 12 are to be answered SOLELY on the basis of the following passage.

The cost approach is used by assessors mainly in valuing one-family homes and properties of a special nature which are not commonly bought and sold and do not produce an income.

There are three aspects to the cost approach to valuation. The first is the actual cost of construction. Where the property has recently been built, the cost of constructing the property is relevant. It, however, may not be a true test as to its value. The building may have been constructed so as to serve the special needs of the owner. What it costs to construct may not truly reflect its value; it may be worth more or less. If it is income-producing property, the income may be more or less than expected. It may be sold for more or less than it cost to build.

The second aspect is replacement cost and applies to older structures. It involves the construction of a similar type of building with the same purpose. It does not require the use of the same materials or design.

Reproduction cost is the third aspect, and it also applies to older structures. It involves construction with the exact same materials and design. The cost in the two latter aspects is construction at today's prices with an allowance made for depreciation from the day the original building was constructed.

9. According to the above passage, which one of the following is a CORRECT statement concerning the cost approach to valuation?
   A. In determining value by the replacement and reproduction cost methods, an allowance must be made for depreciation from the day the building was originally constructed.
   B. The cost approach method is the best method to apply in valuing an office building.
   C. When a structure has been recently built, its actual cost is the best method of determining its value.
   D. The fact that a structure has been built to meet the special needs of the occupant is a relevant factor in valuation.

10. An assessor, in valuing a ten-year-old apartment house, finds that its original construction cost was $1,200,000. In capitalizing its net income, he realizes a valuation of $800,000. In using the replacement cost method and allowing for depreciation, the assessor arrives at a valuation of $900,000.
    According to the above passage, which one of the following valuations is LEAST acceptable for this apartment house?
    A. $1,200,000   B. $800,000
    C. $900,000   D. $850,000

11. The construction cost of a recently built structure is relevant to value, but may not be a true test of value. According to the above passage, which one of the following statements CORRECTLY explains why this is true?
    A. The builder may not know how to construct economically.
    B. A building can depreciate very quickly.
    C. The building may have been built to satisfy certain unique specifications.
    D. Cost-of-construction is not an accepted method of valuation.

12. According to the above passage, which one of the following statements CORRECTLY defines the essential difference between the replacement cost and reproduction cost aspects of the cost approach?

    A. Replacement cost is used only in assessing older buildings; reproduction cost is used only when the building has been recently constructed.
    B. Reproduction cost does not include any allowance for depreciation; replacement cost allows for depreciation from the date of construction of the original building.
    C. Replacement cost involves construction with the same exact materials; reproduction cost does not require the use of the same materials.
    D. Reproduction cost involves construction with the exact same materials and design; replacement cost does not require the use of the same materials and design.

12._____

Questions 13-18.

DIRECTIONS: Questions 13 through 18 are to be answered SOLELY on the basis of the following passage.

Realty, because of fixity in investment, immobility in location, and necessity for shelter purposes, lends itself readily to economic controls when such are deemed essential to serve social or political ends, or where the interest of health, safety, and morality of community population or the nation at large warrants it. Realty has consistently been recognized as a form of private property which is sufficiently invested with public interest to warrant its control either under the police power of a sovereign state and its branches of government or by direct and statutory legislation enacted within the framework of the governmental constitution.

Whenever war or catastrophe causes a sudden shifting of population or suspension of building operations, or both, an imbalance is brought about in the supply and demand for housing. This imbalance in housing demand and supply creates conditions of insecurity and instability among the tenants who fear indiscriminate eviction or unwarranted upward rental adjustments. It is this background of possible exploitation during times of economic stress and strain that underlies the enactment of emergency rent control legislation.

Although rent control has been in effect in many communities, particularly the larger metropolitan communities, since the end of World War II, the attitude of all levels of government is to view this form of legislation as temporary and to hasten, as far as their power permits, a return to normal relations between landlords and tenants.

13. According to the above passage, the reason that realty can conveniently be subjected to controls is due to

    A. public interest   B. site immobility
    C. population shifts   D. moral considerations

13._____

14. The above passage includes as a justification for the imposition of economic controls all of the following EXCEPT

    A. threats to physical safety
    B. socio-political considerations
    C. dangers to health in the community
    D. requirements of police powers

14._____

15. According to the above passage, a LIKELY cause for a cessation of construction might be a
    A. natural disaster
    B. change in the demand for housing
    C. change in the supply of housing
    D. demographic fluctuations

16. According to the above passage, of the following, a tenant's insecurity would MOST likely result in his fear of
    A. reduction in necessary services
    B. loss in equity
    C. rent increases
    D. condemnation proceedings

17. According to the above passage, indiscriminate evictions by landlords during periods of economic difficulties constitute
    A. unlawful acts   B. justifiable measures
    C. desirable actions D. exploitation of tenants

18. According to the above passage, economic controls of realty have been in effect on a widespread basis since
    A. 1918   B. 1945
    C. 1953   D. 1964

Questions 19-22.

DIRECTIONS: Questions 19 through 22 are to be answered SOLELY on the basis of the following passage.

In capitalizing the net income of property to produce a value, certain expenses are permitted to be deducted from gross income. Even though the premises may be fully rented, it is proper to deduct from the gross income an allowance for vacancy. All expenses attributable to the maintenance and upkeep of the premises are deductible. These include heat, light and power, water and sewers, wages or employees and expenses attributable to wages, insurance, repairs and maintenance, supplies and materials, legal and accounting fees, telephone, rental commission, advertising, and so forth. If the premises are furnished, a reserve for the depreciation of personal property is deductible. A capital improvement to the building is not a deductible expense. Real estate taxes should not be deducted as an expense. Instead, taxes should be factored as part of the overall capitalization rate.

It is proper to allow an expense for management of the building even in cases where the owner himself is manager. But payments of interest and principal of the mortgage are not a properly deductible expense. Real property is appraised free and clear of all encumbrances. Otherwise, two identical buildings located next to each other might be valued differently because one has a greater mortgage than the other.

19. According to the above passage, the one of the following which is NOT a proper deductible expense during the year in which the expense is incurred is the cost for
    A. advertising to rent the premises
    B. accounting fees
    C. utilities
    D. putting in central air conditioning

20. According to the above passage, the one of the following statements concerning deductible expenses which is CORRECT is that
    A. a vacancy allowance is a proper deductible expense even though the premises may be fully rented
    B. real estate taxes are a proper deductible expense
    C. if the owner manages his own property, he cannot charge a management fee as a deductible expense
    D. payments for interest and principal of the mortgage are proper deductible expenses

21. According to the above passage, two identical adjacent buildings CANNOT receive different valuations because of differences in their
    A. mortgages   B. net income
    C. leases   D. management fees

22. According to the above passage, an owner of furnished premises may set aside a reserve as a deductible expense for all of the following EXCEPT
    A. refrigerators   B. carpeting
    C. bookcases   D. walls

Questions 23-25.

DIRECTIONS: Questions 23 through 25 are to be answered SOLELY on the basis of the following passage.

The standard for assessment in the state is contained in Section 306 of the Real Property Tax Law. It states that all real property in each assessing unit shall be assessed at the full value thereof. However, the courts of the state have not required assessors to assess at 100% of full value. Assessments of property for real estate tax purposes at less than full value are not invalid if they are made at a uniform percentage of full value throughout the assessing district. In assessing real property, full value is equivalent to market value.

In determining market value of real property for tax purposes, every element which can reasonably affect value of property ought to be considered, and the main considerations should be given to actual sales of the subject or similar property, cost to produce or reproduce the property, capitalization of income therefrom, and the combination of these factors.

23. According to the above passage, the one of the following statements which is INCORRECT is that all real property in each assessing unit
    A. must be assessed at full value
    B. shall be assessed at full value or at a uniform percentage of full value
    C. may be assessed at 50% of full value
    D. may be assessed at 100% of full value

24. According to the above passage, the one of the following elements of value which should be given the LEAST consideration in determining market value is
    A. actual or comparable sales
    B. reproduction cost
    C. amount of mortgage
    D. capitalization of income

25. According to the above passage, the basis for the legality of assessing units, making assessments at a uniform percentage of full value rather than at full value is
    A. Section 306 of the Real Property Tax Law
    B. decisions of the state courts
    C. judgments of individual assessors
    D. decisions of municipal executives

KEY (CORRECT ANSWERS)

1.	A	11.	C
2.	C	12.	D
3.	B	13.	B
4.	B	14.	D
5.	D	15.	A
6.	D	16.	C
7.	C	17.	D
8.	D	18.	B
9.	A	19.	D
10.	A	20.	A

21.	A
22.	D
23.	A
24.	C
25.	B

TEST 3

DIRECTIONS: Each question or incomplete statement is followed by several suggested answers or completions. Select the one that BEST answers the question or completes the statement. *PRINT THE LETTER OF THE CORRECT ANSWER IN THE SPACE AT THE RIGHT.*

Questions 1-4.

DIRECTIONS: Questions 1 through 4 are to be answered SOLELY on the basis of the following passage.

Although zoning is a phase of city planning and is concerned with land use control of private property, zoning powers are better known and more generally applied than most city planning powers. Zoning powers predict the formulation of a master plan and even the formation of the planning commission itself. The widespread application of zoning powers is evident from a survey conducted by the International City Managers' Association. As reported in the 2015 MUNICIPAL YEARBOOK, 98 percent of all cities in excess of ten thousand population had enacted comprehensive zoning ordinances governing the utilization of privately owned land. Since 60 percent of all urban land is generally held under private ownership, the impact of zoning laws upon income and value of real property is most significant.

1. According to the above passage, in relation to the powers of city planning, zoning powers are
    A. not as familiar to the general public
    B. formulated subsequent to the establishment of the powers of the planning commission
    C. more general in their application
    D. likely to develop as a result of the community's master plan

2. According to the above passage, if there are 200 cities in the United States with a population exceeding 10,000 persons, the number of such cities LIKELY to have enacted comprehensive zoning laws is
    A. 190   B. 192
    C. 194   D. 196

3. According to the above passage, for each 400 acres of urban land, it is LIKELY that the amount of land which would be privately owned would be _____ acres.
    A. 220   B. 240
    C. 260   D. 280

4. Of the following, the one whose land use is MOST likely to be affected by zoning controls, according to the above passage, is
    A. Sears Department Store
    B. the Port Authority terminal
    C. the New York Public Library at 42nd Street
    D. the Federal Building

Questions 5-7.

DIRECTIONS: Questions 5 through 7 are to be answered SOLELY on the basis of the following passage.

Apartments located in rehabilitated old law tenement houses are designated as *off-site apartments*. The purpose of such apartments is to provide temporary housing accommodations for the relocation of persons and families living on sites which are to be used for future housing projects who can not otherwise be relocated. A family shall be permitted to continue to occupy an off-site apartment for a period of two years from the date of its admission and shall be required to move out at the termination of such two-year period. However, no proceedings shall be undertaken to remove any tenant now in occupancy of an off-site apartment until after May 9, 2015.

A family shall, however, be required to remove from an off-site apartment prior to the expiration of the periods and date enumerated above if it refuses to accept an available apartment in a public housing project for which it is eligible; or, as a tenant in occupancy, it fails to execute any lease required by management or it fails to comply with other requirements, standard procedures, or rules promulgated by management.

5. A tenant occupying an off-site apartment refuses to renew his lease for one year because he expects to move into a new apartment house within six months. This tenant may
    A. be required to move before his new apartment is ready
    B. be required to move before his new apartment is ready only if his occupancy in the off-site apartment exceeds two years
    C. not be required to move before his new apartment is ready
    D. not be required to move prior to May 9, 2015

6. According to the above passage, if a family living on a site can be relocated to an apartment in a public housing project, it is
    A. eligible for an off-site apartment near its present dwelling
    B. not eligible for any off-site apartment
    C. eligible for an off-site apartment if it has been living in its present home for at least two years
    D. permitted to continue in occupancy for at least two more years

7. According to the above passage, a tenant admitted to an off-site apartment on October 1, 2013 is FIRST subject to removal after
    A. October 1, 2015
    B. May 9, 2015
    C. he has been investigated and found to be ineligible for an apartment in the public housing project
    D. he refuses to sign a lease on the apartment or after September 30, 2015, whichever comes first

Questions 8-14.

DIRECTIONS: Questions 8 through 14 are to be answered SOLELY on the basis of the following passage.

From a nationwide point of view, the need for new housing units during the years immediately ahead will be determined by four major factors. The most important factor is the net change in household formations -- that is, the difference between the number of new households that are formed and the number of existing households that are dissolved, whether by death or other circumstances. During the 2010's, as the children born during the '80's and 90's come of age and marry, the total number of households is expected to increase at a rate of more than 1,000,000 annually. The second factor affecting the need for new housing units is *removals* -- that is, existing units that are demolished, damaged beyond repair, or otherwise removed from the housing supply. A third factor is the number of existing vacancies. To some extent, vacancies can satisfy the housing demand caused by increases in total number of households or by removals, although population shifts that are already underway mean that some areas will have a surfeit of vacancies and other areas will be faced with serious shortages of housing. A final factor, and one that has only recently assumed major importance, is the increasing demand for second homes. These may take any form from a shack in the woods for a city dweller to a pied-a-terre in the city for a suburbanite. Whatever the form, however, it is certain that increasing leisure time, rising amounts of discretionary income, and improvements in transportation are leading more and more Americans to look on a second home not as a rich man's luxury but as the common man's right.

8. The above passage uses the term *housing units* to refer to
    A. residences of all kinds
    B. apartment buildings only
    C. one-family houses only
    D. the total number of families in the United States

9. The above passage uses the word *removals* to mean
    A. the shift of population from one area to another
    B. vacancies that occur when families move
    C. financial losses suffered when a building is damaged or destroyed
    D. former dwellings that are demolished or can no longer be used for housing

10. The expression *pied-a-terre* appears in the next-to-last sentence in the above passage.
    A person who is not familiar with the expression should be able to tell from the way it is used here that it PROBABLY means
    A. a suburban home owned by a commuter
    B. a shack in the woods
    C. a second home that is used from time to time
    D. overnight lodging for a traveler in a strange city

11. Of the factors described in the above passage as having an important influence on the demand for housing, which factor, taken alone, is LEAST likely to encourage the construction of new housing?
    The
    A. net change in household formations
    B. destruction of existing housing
    C. existence of vacancies
    D. use of second homes

12. Based on the above passage, the TOTAL increase in the number of households during the 2010's is expected to be MOST NEARLY
    A. 1,000,000   B. 10,000,000
    C. 100,000,000   D. 1,000,000,000

13. Which one of the following conclusions could MOST logically be drawn from the information given in the above passage?
    A. The population of the United States is increasing at the rate of about 1,000,000 people annually.
    B. There is already a severe housing shortage in all parts of the country.
    C. The need for additional housing units is greater in some parts of the country than in others.
    D. It is still true that only wealthy people can afford to keep up more than one home.

14. Which one of the following conclusions could NOT logically be drawn from the information given in the above passage?
    A. The need for new housing will be even greater in the 2020's than in the 2010's.
    B. Demolition of existing housing must be taken into account in calculating the need for new housing construction.
    C. Having a second home is more common today than it was in the 1970's.
    D. Part of the housing needs of the 2010's can be met by vacancies.

Questions 15-18.

DIRECTIONS: Questions 15 through 18 are to be answered SOLELY on the basis of the following passage.

A city may expand by growing vertically through the replacement of lower buildings with higher ones; or by filling in open spaces between settled areas; or by extending the existing settled area. When the settled area is expanded, growth may take several forms, the most important forms being concentric circle or ring growth around the central nucleus; axial growth, with prongs or fingerlike extensions moving out along main transportation routes; and suburban growth, with the establishment of islands of settlements before the expansion of the main city area. These types of expansion are characteristic of most large cities. Baltimore was for a long time a good example of ring growth, whereas New York, Chicago, and Detroit illustrate axial and suburban growth.

15. The title that BEST expresses the theme of the above passage is
    A. FORMS OF CITY EXPANSION
    B. MAJOR METROPOLITAN PROBLEMS
    C. METHODS OF URBAN PLANNING
    D. SUBURBAN GROWTH IN AMERICA

16. The one of the following which is an example of vertical growth is the
    A. settlement of year-round residents along the upper Hudson River
    B. restoration of former rooming houses to their original brownstone condition
    C. subdivision of large estates into small lot semidetached houses
    D. erection of the Empire State Building in New York City

17. A city that grew as a concentric circle is
    A. Baltimore   B. New York
    C. Chicago   D. Detroit

18. When the author speaks of axial growth, he refers to a situation where
    A. expansion is primarily into rural areas until suburbs are thereby created
    B. small towns and villages are consolidated by gradually growing until one large city is created
    C. the direction in which a city expands is determined by the location of major highways
    D. the number of new buildings is greater than the number of old buildings demolished

18._____

Questions 19-21.

DIRECTIONS: Questions 19 through 21 are to be answered SOLELY on the basis of the following passage.

Incentive zoning is an affirmative tool that has widespread applications. The Zoning Resolution which became effective in 1998 substantially reduced the amount of floor space that a developer could put up on a given size lot and increased the light and air. In the Trump Building, which was built under the old legislation, the floor space is 27 times the size of the lot. The maximum ratio allowed for buildings now without a special permit is 18.

The 1998 zoning ordinance provided incentives to developers to devote part of the plot to public plazas or arcades. This space is needed to supplement the sidewalks, which in many cases are as narrow as they were when the midtown area was lined with brownstone or brickfront houses.

While the newer zoning has produced plazas, it has not of itself proved to be a sufficient development control. Stretches of Third Avenue and the Avenue of the Americas, for example, have been almost completely redeveloped in the last few years. This massive private investment has produced several fine individual buildings. The total environment produced, however, has been disappointing in a number of respects, and there is nowhere near the amenity that there could have been.

19. According to the above passage, the use of incentive zoning has NOT been entirely successful because it
    A. has discouraged redevelopment
    B. has encouraged massive private development along Third Avenue
    C. has been ineffective in controlling overall redevelopment
    D. has not significantly increased the number of parks and plazas being built

19._____

20. According to the above passage, one might conclude that before the 1998 Zoning Resolution was passed,
    A. buildings on a given site were required to have greater setbacks
    B. the amount of private investment in development was significantly smaller than it is today
    C. no controls on development existed
    D. the provision of parks and plazas was less frequent

20._____

21. In the context of the above passage, the word *amenity* means
    A. compliance with regulations
    B. correction of undesirable environmental aspects
    C. responsiveness to guidelines and incentives
    D. pleasant or desirable features

Questions 22-24.

DIRECTIONS: Questions 22 through 24 are to be answered SOLELY on the basis of the following passage.

Physical design plays a very significant role in crime rate. Crime rate has been found to increase almost proportionately with building height. The average number of crimes is much greater in higher buildings than in lower ones (equal to or less than six stories). What is most interesting is that in buildings of six stories or less, the project size or total number of units does not make a difference. It seems that although larger projects encourage crime by fostering feelings of anonymity, isolation, irresponsibility, and lack of identity with surroundings, evidence indicates that larger projects encompassed in low buildings seem to offset what we may assume to be factors conducive to high crime rates. High-rise projects not only experience a higher rate of crime within the buildings, but a greater proportion of the crime occurs in the interior public spaces of these buildings as compared with those of the lower buildings. Lower buildings have more limited public space than higher ones. A criminal probably perceives that the interior public areas of buildings are where his victims are most vulnerable and where the possibility of his being seen or apprehended is minimal. Placement of elevators, entrance lobbies, fire stairs, and secondary exits all are factors related to the likelihood of crimes taking place in buildings. The study of all of these elements should bear some weight in the planning of new projects.

22. According to the above passage, which of the following BEST describes the relationship between building size and crime?
    A. Larger projects lead to a greater crime rate.
    B. Higher buildings tend to increase the crime rate.
    C. The smaller the number of project apartments in low buildings, the higher the crime rate.
    D. Anonymity and isolation serve to lower the crime rate in small buildings.

23. According to the above passage, the likelihood of a criminal attempting a mugging in the interior public portions of a high-rise building is GOOD because
    A. tenants will be constantly flowing in and out of the area
    B. there is easy access to fire stairs and secondary exits
    C. there is a good chance that no one will see him
    D. tenants may not recognize the victims of crime as their neighbors

24. Which of the following is IMPLIED by the above passage as an explanation for 24._____
the fact that the crime rate is lower in large low-rise housing projects than in
large high-rise projects?
   A. Tenants know each other better and take a greater interest in what
      happens in the project.
   B. There is more public space where tenants are likely to gather
      together.
   C. The total number of units in a low-rise project is fewer than the total
      number of units in a high-rise project.
   D. Elevators in low-rise buildings travel quickly, thus limiting the amount
      of time in which a criminal can act.

25. The financing of housing represents two distinct forms of costs. One is the 25._____
actual capital invested, and the other is the interest rate which is charged for
the use of capital. In fixing rents, the interest rate which capital is expected to
yield plays a very important part. On the basis of this statement, it would be
MOST correct to state that
   A. the financing of housing represents two distinct forms of capital
      investment
   B. reducing the interest rate charged for the use of capital is not as
      important as economies in construction in achieving lower rentals
   C. in fixing rents, the interest rate is expected to yield capital gains,
      justifying the investment
   D. the actual capital invested and the interest rate charged for use of
      this capital are factors in determining housing costs

KEY (CORRECT ANSWERS)

1.	C	11.	C
2.	D	12.	B
3.	B	13.	C
4.	A	14.	A
5.	A	15.	A
6.	B	16.	D
7.	D	17.	A
8.	A	18.	C
9.	D	19.	C
10.	C	20.	D

21.	D
22.	B
23.	C
24.	A
25.	D

EXAMINATION SECTION
TEST 1

DIRECTIONS: Each question or incomplete statement is followed by several suggested answers or completions. Select the one that BEST answers the question or completes the statement. *PRINT THE LETTER OF THE CORRECT ANSWER IN THE SPACE AT THE RIGHT.*

1. Our number system has a base of 1.____
   A. 2 B. 5 C. 10 D. 60

2. To find the average weight of the football team, 2.____
   A. add and divide
   B. multiply
   C. add
   D. divide the weight of each player

3. The thermometer used to measure the temperature of a school is called 3.____
   A. Centigrade
   B. Fahrenheit
   C. fever thermometer
   D. gauge

4. The value of a fraction is changed when the same number is _____ to both numerator and denominator. 4.____
   A. added
   B. divided
   C. multiplied
   D. reduced to both terms of the fraction

5. Stores buy their merchandise from firms called 5.____
   A. commissioners
   B. retail firms
   C. factories
   D. wholesale firms

6. The amount of money you borrow is called the 6.____
   A. amount
   B. discount
   C. principal
   D. bank discount

7. An angle of 75° is called a(n) _____ angle. 7.____
   A. acute B. obtuse C. straight D. right

8. The rate of interest could be found by the formula 8.____
   A. $I = Prt$ B. $r = i/pt$ C. $r = Pt$ D. $I = P/Rt$

9. If three sides of one triangle are equal to the three sides of the other, the triangles are 9.____
   A. equilateral
   B. right triangles
   C. scalene
   D. congruent

119

2 (#1)

10. A rectangular solid could be called a(n) 10._____
    A. plane
    B. irregular figure
    C. polygon
    D. prism

11. A written promise to repay the face of a loan is a 11._____
    A. refund
    B. promissory note
    C. dividend
    D. deposit

12. The ² written above the s in the formula As² means 12._____
    A. 2s
    B. s × s
    C. s + s
    D. s/2

13. Selling price includes cost plus profit plus 13._____
    A. expenses
    B. profit
    C. loss
    D. net price

14. When numbers are used to express how many or how much of units of measure, they are called 14._____
    A. digits
    B. denominate numbers
    C. integers
    D. whole numbers

15. The square of a number is that number multiplied by 15._____
    A. two
    B. twice the number
    C. four
    D. itself

16. When the merchant permits the customer to make a down payment and make regular payments on an article, this form of payment is called 16._____
    A. dues
    B. rent
    C. installment buying
    D. utility payments

17. Circles that have a common center and different radii are _____ circles. 17._____
    A. equal
    B. center
    C. congruent
    D. concentric

18. The United States standard of measure of length is the 18._____
    A. base 10
    B. meter
    C. English system
    D. metric system

19. If you put money to work for you, the income you receive is called 19._____
    A. income taxes
    B. interest
    C. bank discount
    D. sales tax

20. A fraction whose numerator is a fraction and denominator is an integer is a _____ fraction. 20._____
    A. common
    B. decimal
    C. improper
    D. complex

KEY (CORRECT ANSWERS)

1.	C	11.	B
2.	A	12.	B
3.	B	13.	A
4.	A	14.	B
5.	D	15.	D
6.	C	16.	C
7.	A	17.	D
8.	B	18.	C
9.	D	19.	B
10.	D	20.	D

SOLUTIONS TO PROBLEMS

1. 10 is the base of our number system. Ex: $456 = (4)(10^2) + (5)(10) + 6$.

2. To find the average weight, add and divide.

3. Fahrenheit degrees would be used for schools.

4. A fraction will change when the same number is added to both numerator and denominator. Ex: Add 5 to both parts of 2/3 to get /8, and 7/8 ≠ 2/3.

5. Stores buy merchandise from wholesale firms.

6. Principal = amount of money borrowed.

7. 75° is an acute angle since it is less than 90°.

8. $R = I/(PT)$ shows rate in terms of interest, principal, and time.

9. If 3 sides of one triangle match 3 sides of a second triangle, they are congruent (SSS).

10. A rectangular solid is a special kind of prism.

11. Promissory note = written promise to repay a loan.

12. $s^2 = s \times s$

13. Selling price includes cost, profit, and expenses.

14. Denominate numbers express units of measure. Ex: 8 gallons.

15. Square of any number = that number times itself. Ex: $4^2 = 4 \times 4 = 16$.

16. Installment buying = down payment + regular payments. Ex: $1000 down payment + $300 payment per month for 2 years.

17. Concentric circles have a common center but different radii. Diagram appears as: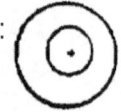

18. The English system is the U.S. standard measure of length. This includes inches, feet, yards, miles, etc.

19. Interest = income received when money is put to work (invested).

20. A complex fraction would contain a fraction within its numerator, denominator, or both.

Ex 1: $\dfrac{\frac{1}{2}}{\frac{1}{3}} = \dfrac{1}{2} \cdot \dfrac{3}{1} = \dfrac{3}{2}$

Ex 2: $\dfrac{1/2}{3} = \dfrac{1}{2} \cdot \dfrac{1}{3} = \dfrac{1}{6}$

Ex 3: $\dfrac{\frac{1}{2}}{3} = \dfrac{1}{1} \cdot \dfrac{3}{2} = \dfrac{3}{2}$

TEST 2

DIRECTIONS: Each question or incomplete statement is followed by several suggested answers or completions. Select the one that BEST answers the question or completes the statement. *PRINT THE LETTER OF THE CORRECT ANSWER IN THE SPACE AT THE RIGHT.*

1. Sally is going to Chicago for a visit. The bus fare is $27.85 one way or a round-trip ticket would be $51.56.
   How much can Sally save by buying a round-trip ticket rather than two one-way tickets?
   A. $4.20
   B. $2.07
   C. $4.14
   D. None of the above

   1.____

2. The Webster Junior High School collected $226.45 for Junior Red Cross and $420.55 for the Community Chest. There were 850 students in the school.
   To the NEAREST cent, what was the average contribution?
   A. $.76
   B. $.50
   C. $1.00
   D. None of the above

   2.____

3. Jack borrowed $57.50 from his father and agreed to pay it in twelve monthly payments of $5.00 each.
   How much interest did he pay?
   A. $2.50
   B. $3.50
   C. $7.50
   D. None of the above

   3.____

4. Joe's mother bought a roast weighing 6 ¾ lbs. at 89¢ a pound.
   How much change did she receive from a $10.00 bill?
   A. $3.99
   B. $5.01
   C. $6.01
   D. None of the above

   4.____

5. The Athletic Department paid $45 total tax on 1,000 tickets.
   How much tax was this per ticket?
   A. $.22
   B. $.45
   C. 4.5 cents
   D. None of the above

   5.____

6. Mary bought 4½ yards of lace. She used $1^2/_3$ yards of it on a blouse.
   _____ yards of lace were left.
   A. $3\,^1/_6$
   B. 3 ½
   C. $2\,^5/_6$
   D. None of the above

   6.____

7. The girls are going to make aprons for Junior Red Cross. The pattern calls for ¾ yard of material for one apron.
   They will need _____ yards for 25 aprons.
   A. 33 $^1/_3$
   B. 18 ¾
   C. 20
   D. None of the above

   7.____

2 (#2)

8. Which city on a world map of standard time zones would be NEAR the 75°W? 8.____
   A. Greenwich B. Sydney
   C. Calcutta D. None of the above

9. John's father made a down payment on a car and has $1,320 left to pay. 9.____
   He pays $55 each month.
   It will take him _____ months to finish the car payments.
   A. 42 B. 24
   C. 18 D. None of the above

10. Pete bought a board 12 ft. 8 in. long from which he wants to make three shelves. 10.____
    Two of the shelves are 2 ft. 8 in. long, and the third shelf is 1 ft. 6 in. long.
    How long will the piece be that is left over?
    A. 5 ft. 8 in. B. 5 ft. 10 in.
    C. 6 ft. 10 in. D. None of the above

11. A factory worker received an increase of 15% in his hourly wages. His former 11.____
    wages were $1.80 per hour.
    How much a week did his wages INCREASE in a forty-hour week?
    A. $21.17 B. $8.00
    C. $10.80 D. None of the above

12. Find the installment price of a washing machine if the down payment is 12.____
    $39.90, the monthly payments are $14.13 for twelve months, and the interest
    charge is $9.86.
    A. $179.52 B. $219.42
    C. $169.56 D. None of the above

13. How many hundreds in 18762? 13.____
    A. 7 B. 87
    C. 187 D. None of the above

14. The football team won 16 games and lost 4 games. 14.____
    What percent of the games played did they win?
    A. 75% B. 80%
    C. 40% D. None of the above

15. The bakery boxed doughnuts one half dozen to a box. 15.____
    They will have _____ full boxes if they fry 500 doughnuts.
    A. 41 B. 83
    C. 82 D. None of the above

16. Jane's parents burn fuel oil. They have used 180 gallons. The gauge indicates 16.____
    the tank is 5/8 full.
    The tank holds _____ gallons.
    A. 255 B. 480
    C. 600 D. None of the above

3 (#2)

17. _____ tiles, each a 9" square, could be laid in one width of a recreation room that is 25 feet long and 16½ feet wide.
    A. 22
    B. 149
    C. 51
    D. None of the above

18. The outside diameter of a wheel on Bob's bicycle is 28 inches. The outside diameter of a wheel on his little brother's bicycle is 21 inches. After traveling a mile, the little brother's wheel will make _____ revolutions more.
    A. 1080
    B. 269.5
    C. 240
    D. None of the above

19. Bill gets 17 ¾ miles per gallon.
    At this rate, he should get _____ miles if he buys 5.6 gallons of gasoline.
    A. 317
    B. 99.4
    C. 85
    D. None of the above

20. The scale drawing of a house is 1 in. = 12 ft.
    If a room is 33 feet long, a _____ inch line should be used on the blueprint to represent that distance.
    A. 2 ¾
    B. 3.3
    C. 2.1`
    D. None of the above

21. A 2-inch gear makes 75 revolutions per minute.
    A 3-inch fear makes _____ rpm at the same rate of speed.
    A. 12 ½
    B. 112 ½
    C. 50
    D. None of the above

22. What is the selling price of a radio that cost the dealer $36 and the margin is 40% of the selling price?
    A. $60
    B. $45
    C. $50.40
    None of the above

23. Mr. Jacks used 35 kwh.
    If the charge is 8¢ a kwh for the first 20 kwh and 5¢ for the remainder, what was the TOTAL charge?
    A. $2.35
    B. $3.35
    C. $4.55
    D. None of the above

24. Druggists use a unit of measurement of weight called the grain. There are *approximately* 437.5 grains in one ounce.
    There are APPROXIMATELY _____ grains in a pound.
    A. 7000
    B. 5252
    C. 73,400
    D. None of the above

25. A gasoline tank is 16 ft. high and has a diameter of 14 ft.
    The tank will hold _____ cubic feet of gasoline (use 22/7 for pi) to the NEAREST 10 cu. ft.
    A. 704
    B. 784
    C. 2460
    D. None of the above

KEY (CORRECT ANSWERS)

1. C
2. A
3. A
4. A
5. C

6. C
7. B
8. D
9. B
10. B

11. C
12. B
13. C
14. B
15. B

16. B
17. A
18. C
19. B
20. A

21. C
22. A
23. A
24. A
25. C

5 (#2)

SOLUTIONS TO PROBLEMS

1. Savings = ($27.85)(2) - $51.56 = $4.14

2. Average contribution = ($226.45 + $420.55) ÷ 850 = $647 ÷ 850 ≈ $.76

3. Interest = (12)($5.00) - $57.50 = $2.50

4. $10.00 – (6.75)(.89) = $3.99 change

5. $45 ÷ 1000 = .045 = 4.5 cents tax per ticket

6. 4 1/2 – 1 2/3 = 4 3/6 – 1 4/6 – 1 = 2 5.6 yds, left

7. (3/4)(25) = 18 3/4 yds. needed

8. Refer to world map. None is correct.

9. $1320 ÷ 55 = 24 months

10. 12'8" – 2'8" – 2'8" – 1'6" = 152" – 32" – 32" – 18" = 70" = 5'10"

11. Increase = ($1.80)(.15)(40) = $10.80 per week

12. $39.90 + ($14.13)(12) + $9.96 = $219.42 installment price

13. 18,762 ÷ 100 = 187 with remainder of 62. So, there are 187 hundreds in 18,762.

14. Percent won = 16/20 = 80%

15. 500 ÷ 6 = 83 1/3, which means 83 full boxes + 1/3 of a box

16. 180 gallons represents 3/8 of the entire tank. Thus, the tank's capacity = 180 ÷ 3/8 = 480 gallons

17. 25' = 300" and 16 1/2' = 198". Now, 300 ÷ 9 = 33 1.3 and 198 ÷ 9 = 22. Then the number of tiles that could fit in 1 width = 22. (The actual number of tiles that could fit in the entire room = (22)(33) = 726)

18. 1 revolution of Bob's bicycle = 2π = $(2 \times \frac{22}{7} \times 14)$ = 88"

    1 revolution of his brother's bicycle = 2π = $(2 \times \frac{22}{7} \times 10.5)$ = 66"

6 (#2)

19. $(17\frac{3}{4})(5.6) = (17.75)(5.6) = 99.4$ miles

20. 33 ÷ 12 = 2 3/4-inch line needed.

21. Let x = rpm. 2/3 = x/75. Solving, x = 50.
    Note: Size of gear is inversely related to rpm.

22. Let x = selling price. Then, $36 = .60x. Solving, x = $60.

23. Total charge = (.08)(20) + (.05)(15) = $2.35

24. (437.5)(16) = 7000 grains in a pound (approx.)

25. Volume = $(\pi)(7^2)(16) \approx 2460$ cu. ft.

ARITHMETICAL REASONING
EXAMINATION SECTION
TEST 1

DIRECTIONS: Each question or incomplete statement is followed by several suggested answers or completions. Select the one that BEST answers the question or completes the Statement. *PRINT THE LETTER OF THE CORRECT ANSWER IN THE SPACE AT THE RIGHT.*

1. The weekly pay for 8 hours a day, 5 days a week, at $16.8750 an hour can be calculated as

   A. 5 x 8 x 16.8570
   B. 8 + 5 x 16.8750
   C. 8 x 5 x 16.8750
   D. 8 + 5 x 16.8570

   1.____

2. A bus operator starts out with $10.00 in change, and his fare box indicates he collects $85.50 in passenger fares. On counting his money, he finds he has 75 one dollar bills, 10 fifty cent pieces, 22 quarters, and 70 dimes.
   To have the CORRECT amount, the number of nickels he should have is

   A. 45   B. 50   C. 55   D. 60

   2.____

3. The register on the fare box of a certain bus has 5 dials and shows the total number of cents collected. When a particular bus operator starts his tour of duty, the register reading is 08980, and at the conclusion of his tour of duty the reading is 14540.
   The TOTAL number of 20-cent fares collected during this operator's tour was

   A. 278   B. 598   C. 783   D. 969

   3.____

4. A particular bus has 12 cross seats holding two passengers each, plus rear and longitudinal seats holding a total of 14 additional passengers.
   If the number of standees permitted on a bus is one-half the number of seated passengers, the TOTAL passenger capacity of this bus is

   A. 26   B. 38   C. 39   D. 57

   4.____

5. A crosstown bus operates between two terminals 22 blocks apart and makes 18 stops. It takes half a minute to travel each block and a quarter of a minute at each stop, and 5 minutes are lost at traffic lights.
   The TOTAL time required to go from one terminal to the other is _____ minutes.

   A. 15 1/2   B. 17 1/2   C. 20 1/2   D. 22 1/2

   5.____

6. The TOTAL value of an operator's change fund consisting of 7 half-dollars, 19 quarters, 169 dimes, and 105 nickels is

   A. $28.40   B. $29.40   C. $30.40   D. $31.40

   6.____

7. If it takes a bus 30 seconds to pass two checkpoints that are 500 feet apart, then the speed of the bus is APPROXIMATELY _____ m.p.h.

   A. 10.1   B. 11.4   C. 12.7   D. 14.2

   7.____

8. If the length of a particular bus route is 8.6 miles and the average speed of a bus on this route is 7.5 miles per hour, then the ONE-WAY running time for a bus is _____ minutes.

   A. 52.3   B. 64.5   C. 68.8   D. 75.6

9. If your watch gains 20 minutes per day and you set it to the correct time at 7:00 A.M., the correct time, to the NEAREST minute, when the watch indicates 1:00 P.M. is

   A. 12:50   B. 12:56   C. 1:05   D. 1:10

10. A particular bus seats 34 passengers and stands half that number.
    The TOTAL passenger capacity of the bus is

    A. 41   B. 51   C. 61   D. 68

11. The fare register box on a bus shows the total number of cents collected. At the beginning of a run, the register reading of a certain box was 15750 and at the end of the run the reading was 17150.
    The TOTAL number of $1.00 fares collected during the run was

    A. 16   B. 17   C. 14   D. 19

12. Manuals on driving stress the importance of allowing ample braking distance to the car ahead, the most common rule of thumb being to allow a car length for each ten miles per hour of speed.
    If the overall length of a car is 210 inches, the proper braking distance to allow at a speed of 40 miles per hour is NEAREST to _____ feet.

    A. 700   B. 500   C. 70   D. 50

13. A bus requires 40 minutes to go from one terminal to another and stops for 10 minutes at each terminal. The MAXIMUM number of one-way trips that the bus can complete in 6 hours is

    A. 6   B. 7   C. 8   D. 9

Questions 14-21.

DIRECTIONS: Questions 14 through 21 in Column I are questions of simple arithmetic, each of which has one of the answers listed in Column II. For each item in Column I, select the CORRECT answer from Column II.

COLUMN I	COLUMN II
14. 229 times 9	A. 1,383
15. 11,064 divided by 8	B. 1,752
16. 1,384 plus 368	C. 2,061
17. 3,021 minus 447 minus 386	D. 2,682
18. 149 times 3 times 6	E. 2,188
19. 727 plus 17 plus 639	

20. 2,881 minus 693   20._____

21. 43,281 divided by 3 divided by 7   21._____

Questions 22-25.

DIRECTIONS: Questions 22 through 25 in Column I are questions of simple arithmetic, each of which has one of the answers listed in Column II. For each item in Column I, select the CORRECT answer from Column II.

COLUMN I	COLUMN II	
22. 198 times 3 times 4	A. 1,267	22._____
23. 837 plus 18 plus 412	B. 2,376	23._____
24. 8,869 divided by 7	C. 1,944	24._____
25. 2,693 minus 509	D. 1,867	25._____
	E. 2,184	
	F. 2,076	

KEY (CORRECT ANSWERS)

1.	C		11.	C
2.	D		12.	C
3.	A		13.	B
4.	D		14.	C
5.	C		15.	A
6.	C		16.	B
7.	B		17.	E
8.	C		18.	D
9.	B		19.	A
10.	B		20.	E

21. C
22. B
23. A
24. A
25. E

4 (#1)

SOLUTIONS TO PROBLEMS

1. Weekly pay = 5 x 8 x 16.8750
2. $10.00 + $85.50 - ($75+$5+5.50+$7) = $3 = 60 nickels
3. 14,540 - 08980 = 05560, and 5560 ÷ 20 = 278
4. Number of people sitting = (12)(2) + 14 = 38. Number of people on bus = 38 + (1/2)(38) = 57
5. Total time = (22)(1/2) + (18)(1/4) + 5 = 20.5 minutes
6. (7)(.50) + (19)(.25) + (169)(.10) + (105)(.05) = $30.40
7. 500 ft in 30 sec = 16 2/3 ft per sec. Since 60 mph = 88 ft per sec, the bus' speed = (60)(16 2/3/88) 11.4 mph
8. Let x = number of minutes. Then, 7.5/60 = 8.6/x. Solving, x = 68.8
9. If the watch gains 20 mins. in 24 hrs., it gains 5/6 min. or 50 seconds in 1 hour. In 6 hours, from 7:00 AM to 1:00 PM, it gains 5 mins: (6 x 5/6). When the watch indicates 1:00 PM, the correct time is 12:55 PM.
10. Passenger capacity = 34 + (1/2)(34) = 51
11. 17150 - 15750 = 1400, so 1400 cents = 14 $1 fares
12. (210 in.)(40/10) = 840 in. = 70 ft.
13. 6 hrs. ÷ 5/6 hr. = 7.2, so 7 trips would be the maximum number.
14. (229)(9) = 2061
15. 11,064 ÷ 8 = 1383
16. 1384 + 368 = 1752
17. 3021 - 447 - 386 = 2188
18. (149)(3)(6) = 2682
19. 727 + 17 + 639 = 1383
20. 2881 - 693 = 2188
21. 43,281 ÷ 3 ÷ 7 = 2061
22. (198)(3)(4) = 2376
23. 837 + 18 + 412 = 1267
24. 8869 ÷ 7 = 1267
25. 2693 - 509 = 2184

TEST 2

DIRECTIONS: Each question or incomplete statement is followed by several suggested answers or completions. Select the one that BEST answers the question or completes the statement. *PRINT THE LETTER OF THE CORRECT ANSWER IN THE SPACE AT THE RIGHT.*

1. A bus depot took in $308,645.00 during a 3-month period. During the following 3-month period, the revenue decreased 17%.
   The revenue for the second 3-month period was MOST NEARLY

   A. $333,890.00 B. $283,400.00
   C. $256,175.00 D. $238,655.00

   1._____

2. A surface line dispatcher desires to check the speed of a certain bus.
   If he times the bus as traveling 220 feet in 4.9 seconds, then the bus is traveling at APPROXIMATELY_____ m.p.h.

   A. 20   B. 30   C. 36   D. 44

   2._____

3. If the thickness of material worn from a bus brake lining is approximately .20 inch for every 3,000 miles of wheel travel, then the number of miles the wheel will have traveled to reduce the thickness from .75 inch to .25 inch is

   A. 3,750   B. 6,000   C. 7,500   D. 11,250

   3._____

4. A dispatcher desires to check the speed of a certain 40-foot bus.
   If he times the bus as passing him in 1.5 seconds, then the bus is traveling at APPROXIMATELY_____ m.p.h.

   A. 15   B. 18   C. 22   D. 27

   4._____

5. The number of feet required to bring a bus traveling at 30 m.p.h. to a stop at a braking rate of 3 miles per hour per second is NEAREST to _____ feet.

   A. 180   B. 200   C. 220   D. 240

   5._____

6. A bus leaves one time point at 10:35 and arrives at the next time point at 11:00. If the distance between the time points is 3 miles, the average speed of the bus, in m.p.h., was MOST NEARLY

   A. 6   B. 6 1/2   C. 7   D. 7 1/2

   6._____

7. Eighty percent of the 300 operators in your depot are married, and 50% of all operators are under 35 years of age.
   The MINIMUM number of married operators in this lower age group is

   A. 60   B. 90   C. 150   D. 240

   7._____

8. A bus maintained a speed of 5 m.p.h. for one-third of its route, 10 m.p.h. for the second third, and 15 m.p.h. for the final third.
   The AVERAGE speed for the entire route was CLOSEST to _____ m.p.h.

   A. 8   B. 9   C. 10   D. 11

   8._____

9. During the month of August, approximately 900,000 more passengers used the surface lines than during the same month the year before. This was an increase of about 3%. The total number of passengers who used this surface transportation system during August was NEAREST to

   A. 3,000,000 B. 3,900,000
   C. 29,000,000 D. 31,000,000

10. Assume that there are 300 bus operators at terminal A. Terminal B has 85% as many bus operators as terminal A, and terminal C has 90% as many bus operators as terminal B. The number of operators assigned to terminal C is NEAREST to

    A. 230 B. 245 C. 255 D. 270

11. A bus leaves the terminal on time at 11:48 A.M. and after one roundtrip returns 11 minutes late at 1:06 P.M. It leaves again on time at 1:12 P.M.
    If the scheduled recovery time at both ends of the line is the same, the scheduled terminal-to-terminal running time, in minutes, is

    A. 25 B. 33 C. 42 D. 50

12. A bus line had a schedule headway of 6 minutes. Run #7 left the near terminal at 10:45 A.M. and shortly thereafter had to be taken out of service on account of engine trouble. Its passengers were picked up by its follower, run #8. The delay caused run #8 to arrive at the far terminal 6 minutes late.
    If the time of arrival of run #8 was 11:53 A.M., then the scheduled running time for the trip was _____ minutes.

    A. 44 B. 56 C. 68 D. 96

13. If a fuel storage tank contains 11,200 gallons of fuel when it is 85% full, its MAXIMUM capacity, in gallons, is CLOSEST to

    A. 9,589 B. 13,175 C. 13,274 D. 14,107

14. Assume that a total of 345 people are employed at a certain location.
    If 2/5 of these people report to work at 7:00 A.M. and another 1/5 at 8:00 A.M., then the number of people that have NOT yet reported to work is

    A. 73 B. 138 C. 154 D. 199

15. Assume that a bus consumes an average of 8 gallons of fuel per hour and that each gallon of fuel weighs 7 1/4 pounds.
    In a 6 hour period, the amount of fuel used, in pounds, is

    A. 108 B. 232 C. 348 D. 399

16. The opening Metrocard reading on a daily register is 1,152, and the last Metrocard closing reading is 1,463. The opening cash reading is 12,015, and the last cash closing reading is 24,345. (Reading increases by 30 for each fare.) The total number of revenue-paying passengers that this bus carried on this day is CLOSEST to

    A. 722 B. 1,112 C. 1,463 D. 12,330

17. If it takes a bus 30 seconds to pass two checkpoints that are 500 feet apart, then the speed of the bus is APPROXIMATELY _____ m.p.h.

    A. 10.1 B. 11.4 C. 12.7 D. 14.2

18. If the length of a particular bus route is 8.6 miles and the average speed of a bus on this route is 7.5 miles per hour, then the one-way running time for a bus is _____ minutes.

    A. 52.3 B. 64.5 C. 68.8 D. 75.6

19. A certain bus route is five miles long. The schedule speed for half of the route is 6 m.p.h., and for the other half of the route it is 15 m.p.h.
    The AVERAGE schedule speed for the entire route

    A. is between 6 m.p.h. and 10.5 m.p.h.
    B. is exactly 10.5 m.p.h.
    C. is between 10.5 m.p.h. and 15 m.p.h.
    D. cannot be calculated without knowing running time for each half of the route

20. A regular tour of duty for an operator requires him to report at 5:50 A.M., leave on his first run at 6:05 A.M., swing from 10:30 A.M. to 2:00 P.M., complete his last.
    run at 5:10 P.M., and clear/at 5:20 P.M. (Notpaid ..for swing time.) The normal pay for this tour is at the operator's regular rate for _____ hours, _____ minutes.

    A. 9; 30 B. 9; 45 C. 10; 15 D. 11; 30

21. An employee who has a wristwatch which gains 30 minutes per day sets it to the correct time at 6:00 A.M.
    When the watch indicates 12:00 Noon, the CORRECT time, to the nearest minute, is

    A. 11:46 B. 11:53 C. 12:07 D. 12:14

22. The one-way running time on a bus route is 1 hour and 6 minutes, and the average speed of a bus on this route is 14 m. p.h.
    What is the length, in miles, of this route?

    A. 13.5 B. 14.0 C. 14.4 D. 15.4

23. A bus consumes 45 gallons of fuel after having traveled a distance of 328 miles.
    The number of miles per gallon of fuel that this bus gets, based on this information, is CLOSEST to

    A. 6.8 B. 7.3 C. 7.8 D. 8.3

24. A bus operator with a weekday run whose hourly rate of pay is $12.60 normally reports for work at 7:30 A.M. and clears at 3:00 P.M.(On report days he works until 4 P.M.) What is his gross pay for a day on which he is required to write an accident report at the end of his run?

    A. $107.10 B. $108.90 C. $113.40 D. $115.60

4 (#2)

25. A passenger count was made at a certain terminal between 8 A.M. and 9 A.M., and it was noted that eight buses were loaded with the following number of passengers: 34, 52, 29, 63, 19, 17, 56, and 42, respectively.
The TOTAL number of passengers boarding these eight buses was

    A. 302   B. 312   C. 313   D. 412

25.____

KEY (CORRECT ANSWERS)

1. C   11. A
2. B   12. B
3. C   13. B
4. B   14. B
5. C   15. C

6. C   16. A
7. B   17. B
8. A   18. C
9. D   19. A
10. C   20. B

21. B
22. D
23. B
24. A
25. B

SOLUTIONS TO PROBLEMS

1. $(\$308,645)(.83) \approx \$256,175$

2. 220 ft. in 4.9 sec $\approx$ 45 ft. per sec. Since 60 mph means 88 ft.per sec., the bus is moving at $(60)(45/88) \approx 30$ mph

3. $.75 - .25 = .50$. Then, $(3000)(.50/.20) = 7500$ miles

4. 40 ft. in 1.5 sec. = 26 2/6 ft. per sec. Thus, the bus is moving at $(60)(26\ 2/3\ /88) \approx 18$ mph

5. Initial speed is 30 mph = 44 ft. per sec. Final speed (when fully stopped) is 0 ft. per sec. Average speed = 22 ft. per sec. Distance = (average speed)(time) = (22)(10 sec.) = 220 ft.

6. 3 miles in 25 min. means $(3)(60/25) = 7.2 \approx 7$ mph

7. Let x = minimum number of married operators under 35 years old. Then, 240-x = number of married operators over 35 years old, and 150-x = number of unmarried operators under 35 years old. Since there are probably operators who are neither married nor under 35 years old, $(240-x) + (x) + (150-x) \leq 300$. Solving, $x \geq 90$.

8. 5 mph= 1/3; 10 mph= 1/3; 15 mph= 1/3. 5 + 10 + 15= 30. 30 divided by 3= 10 mph average speed.

9. $900,000 \div .03 = 30,000,000$. Then, $30,000,000 + 900,000 = 30,900,000 \approx 31,000,000$ passengers in August.

10. Terminal B has $(300 \times .85) = 255$ operators, so terminal C has $(255)(.90) \approx 230$ operators.

11. The scheduled running time for a roundtrip from 11:48 AM to 12:55 PM is 67 minutes. Since the recovery time is 17 minutes (12:55 PM - 1:12 PM), and recovery time must only be deducted once from the running time for a roundtrip, the scheduled running time from terminal to terminal is $\frac{67-17}{2} = \frac{50}{2} = 25$

12. From 10:45 AM to 11:53 AM is 68 minutes. Then, 68 - 6 - 6 = 56 minutes for the scheduled running time.

13. $11,200 \div .85 \approx 13,176$, closest to 13,175 gallons

14. $(1 - 2/5 - 1/5)(345) = 138$ people

15. $(6)(8)(7\ 1/4) = 348$ pounds of fuel

16. Number of people paying by Metrocard = 1463 - 1152 = 311 Number of people paying by cash = $(24,345-12,015) \div 30 = 411$ Total of individuals paying revenue = 722

17. 500 ft. in 30 sec. means 16 2/3 ft. per sec. Then, the speed of the bus = $(60)(16\ 2/3 \div 88) \approx 11.4$ mph

18. $8.6 \div 7.5 = 1.14\overline{6}$ hrs. = 68.8 min.

19. Times for each half are $\frac{2.5}{6} = .41\overline{6}$ hrs. and $\frac{2.5}{15} = .1\overline{6}$ min. Average speed $= 5 \div (.41\overline{6} + .1\overline{6}) \approx 8.6$ mph; thus, it is between 6 mph and 10.5 mph.

20. His tour extends from 5:50 AM to 5:20 PM, for a total period of 11 1/2 hours, less swing time from 10:30 AM to 2:00 PM, which is 3 1/2 hours. 11 1/2 - 3 1/2 = 8 hours

21. 30 min/1440 min = $.0208\overline{3}$ gain. Thus, 6 hrs. on the watch indicates
 $6 \div 1.0208\overline{3} \approx 5.88$ hrs. hrs. $\approx$ 5 hrs. 53 min. in actual time. The actual time is 11:53 AM.

22. Let x = miles on this route. Then, $\dfrac{14}{x} = \dfrac{1\,\text{hr.}}{1.10\,\text{hrs.}}$ Solving, x = 15.4

23. $328 \div 45 \approx 7.3$ miles per gallon

24. 7:30 AM to 4:00 PM = 8 1/2 hrs. Then, ($12.60)(8.5) = $107.10

25. 34 + 52 + 29 + 63 + 19 + 17 + 56 + 42 = 312 passengers

TEST 3

DIRECTIONS: Each question or incomplete statement is followed by several suggested answers or completions. Select the one that BEST answers the question or completes the statement. *PRINT THE LETTER OF THE CORRECT ANSWER IN THE SPACE AT THE RIGHT.*

1. The total automobile traffic of a bridge increased from 33,000 to 37,000. This represents an increase of APPROXIMATELY

    A. 8% B. 12% C. 16% D. 20%

2. Eighty percent of the vessels passing under a certain bridge are tugboats. If 105 vessels pass under this bridge daily, the number of tugboats passing under the bridge daily is

    A. 80 B. 84 C. 88 D. 92

3. A certain shelf can safely hold 140 pounds. On the shelf is a 45 pound carton of nuts and bolts, a 52 pound carton of assorted hardware, and two containers of lead paint weighing 27 lbs. each.
The shelf

    A. is overloaded by 16 lbs.
    B. can safely hold an additional 16 lbs.
    C. is overloaded by 11 lbs.
    D. can safely hold an additional 11 lbs.

4. Of the following decimals, the one which has the same value as 3/8 is

    A. 0.125 B. 0.266 C. 0.333 D. 0.375

5. If an iron bar 6'6 1/8" long is cut in half, the length of each piece will then be MOST NEARLY

    A. 3'3 1/16" B. 3'3 1/8"
    C. 3'6 1/8"   D. 3'6 1/4"

6. The amount of liquid that can be stored in 72 one-quart cans is _____ gallons.

    A. 9 B. 18 C. 24 D. 36

7. Suppose that an officer carried two packages, one weighing 73 pounds and the other weighing 41 pounds 3 ounces.
The DIFFERENCE between the weights of the two packages was _____ pounds _____ ounces.

    A. 31; 5 B. 31; 13 C. 32; 6 D. 32; 12

8. Suppose that the toll money collected at a bridge during March of last year was $153,696.
If the toll money collected at this bridge in April was 3% higher than in March, then the April total was MOST NEARLY

    A. $149,085 B. $158,307 C. $167,431 D. $200,075

9. Suppose that 10% more vehicles crossed a certain bridge on Friday than on the previous day.
   If 18,100 cars, 1,290 trucks, and 130 buses used the bridge on Thursday, how many cars, trucks, and buses crossed the bridge on Friday?

   A. 17,568   B. 18,144   C. 19,520   D. 21,472

10. The maximum height allowed for vehicles using a particular bridge under normal conditions is 13 feet 6 inches.
    If a vehicle is 15 feet 5 inches tall, by exactly what amount does the vehicle EXCEED the maximum height limit for this bridge?
    _____ foot(feet) _____ inch(es).

    A. 1; 9   B. 1; 11   C. 2; 1   D. 2; 3

11. The number of cars, trucks, and buses using two different toll lanes on a certain day was as follows:

	Lane 1	Lane 2
Cars	994	1,086
Trucks	113	51
Buses	31	16

    A comparison of these two lanes would show that the TOTAL number of cars, trucks, and buses using Lane 1 on that day was _____ than the total at Lane 2.

    A. 15 fewer   B. 25 fewer   C. 15 more   D. 25 more

12. A certain officer was assigned to collect tolls for two hours. The officer was given $80 in various bills and $150 in quarters so that he could make change. He placed this money in a drawer in the toll booth. At the end of the two hours of toll collecting, the officer had a total of $1,375.75 in the drawer.
    The percent of this total which represents the tolls collected is MOST NEARLY

    A. 15%   B. 63%   C. 78%   D. 83%

13. The number of vehicles using a particular lane each hour during a 6-hour period varied as follows: 134, 210, 213, 234, 111, and 118.
    The AVERAGE number of vehicles per hour using the toll lane during this period was

    A. 150   B. 160   C. 170   D. 180

14. Assume that you have been assigned to a shift which begins at 2:00 P.M., and you want to arrive 10 minutes before the shift begins. If you average 28 miles per hour while driving to work and must travel 21 miles, at exactly what time should you start driving to work?

    A. 12:30 P.M.   B. 12:40 P.M.
    C. 1:05 P.M.   D. 1:15 P.M.

15. A rectangular storage room is 15 ft. by 16 ft., and the ceiling height is 10 feet.
    The volume of this room, in cubic feet, is

    A. 2,200   B. 2,300   C. 2,400   D. 2,500

16. One-quarter of the 168 light bulbs on a certain bridge are replaced during the year. If these bulbs cost the city 21 cents each, the yearly cost of replacing the bulbs is

    A. $8.40   B. $8.82   C. $8.86   D. $8.92

    16.____

17. If 14,229 is divided by 17, the answer is

    A. 737   B. 747   C. 837   D. 847

    17.____

18. A worker receives $171.50 per day.
    In 15 working days, his TOTAL earnings should be

    A. $2,560.50   B. $2,562.50
    C. $2,570.50   D. $2,572.50

    18.____

19. If an Assistant Bridge Operator earns $24,500 in the first six months of a year and receives a 10% raise in salary for the next six months of the same year, his total earnings for the year will be

    A. $50,900   B. $51,450   C. $52,750   D. $53,950

    19.____

20. The area of the metal plate shown at the right, minus the hole area, is MOST NEARLY _____ square inches.
    A. 8.5
    B. 8.9
    C. 9.4
    D. 10.1

    20.____

21. The percentage of the tank shown at the right that is filled with water is MOST NEARLY
    A. 33
    B. 35
    C. 37
    D. 39

    21.____

22. Assume that a sump pit measures 10 feet long, 10 feet wide, and 12 feet deep. If each cubic foot of water is equal to 7.5 gallons, the amount of water in the sump when half full will be MOST NEARLY _____ gallons.

    A. 120   B. 1,200   C. 4,500   D. 9,000

    22.____

23. If the water in a sump pit is 10 feet deep, the pressure at the bottom of the pit, in lbs. per sq. in., exerted by the water is MOST NEARLY (assuming water weighs 62.4 lbs./cu. ft.)

    A. 4.3   B. 52   C. 62.4   D. 624

    23.____

24. If part of a walkway measuring 9 feet by 20 feet is to be replaced by concrete 6 inches thick, the cubic yards of concrete needed is MOST NEARLY

    A. 1 1/2   B. 3 1/2   C. 42   D. 90

    24.____

25. A new bridge spanning a river is expected to carry 60,000 cars a day on a rainy day and 80,000 cars a day on other kinds of days.
   If there is a $1 toll and one chance in four of a rainy day, the expected value of a day's revenue is

   A. $35,000   B. $75,000   C. $95,000   D. $140,000

KEY (CORRECT ANSWERS)

1. B
2. B
3. C
4. D
5. A

6. B
7. B
8. B
9. D
10. B

11. A
12. D
13. C
14. C
15. C

16. B
17. C
18. D
19. B
20. B

21. D
22. C
23. A
24. B
25. B

SOLUTIONS TO PROBLEMS

1. $4000 \div 33{,}000 \approx 12\%$

2. $(105)(.80) = 84$ tugboats

3. $140 - 45 - 52 - (2)(27) = -11$, so the shelf is overloaded by 11 lbs.

4. $3/8 = .375$

5. $(6'6\frac{1}{8}") \div 2 = 3'3\frac{1}{16}"$

6. Since 4 quarts = 1 gallon, 72 quarts = 18 gallons

7. 73 lbs. - 41 lbs. 3 oz. = 31 lbs. 13 oz.

8. $(\$153{,}696)(1.03) = \$158{,}307$

9. $(18{,}100+1{,}290+130 \times 1.10) = 21{,}472$ vehicles crossed the bridge on Friday.

10. 15 ft. 5 in. - 13 ft. 6 in. = 1 ft. 11 in.

11. Lane 1 had 1138 vehicles, whereas lane 2 had 1153 vehicles. Lane 1 had 15 fewer vehicles than lane 2.

12. Tolls collected = $\$1375.75 - \$230 = \$1145.75$. Then, $\$1145.75 \div \$1375.75 \approx 83\%$

13. $(134+210+213+234+111+118) \div 6 = 170$ vehicles

14. $21/28 = .75$ hr. Then, 1:50 PM - .75 hr. = 1:05 PM

15. Volume = $(15')(16')(10') = 2400$ cu.ft.

16. Cost = $(.21)(168)(1/4) = \$8.82$

17. $14{,}229 \div 17 = 837$

18. Total earnings = $(\$171.50)(15) = \$2572.50$

19. Total earnings = $\$24{,}500 + (1.10)(\$24{,}500) = \$51{,}450$

20. $(4)(3) - (\pi)(1)^2 = 8.9$ sq.in.

21. $\dfrac{7"}{18"} \approx 39\%$

22. Half the volume = $(1/2)(10)(10)(12) = 600$ cu.ft.
    Then, $(600)(7.5) = 4500$ gallons

23. Since 1728 cu.in. = 1 cu.ft., 62.4 lbs./cu.ft. = $0.36\overline{1}$ lbs./cu.in. With a depth of 10 ft. or 120 in., pressure = $(.0361 \times 120) \approx 4.3$ lbs./in.^{2}

24. $(9')(20')(1/2') = 90$ cu.ft. $= 90/27 = 3\,1/3$ or about $3\,1/2$ cu.yds.

25. $(\$80{,}000)(.75) + (\$60{,}000)(.25) = \$75{,}000$

PREPARING WRITTEN MATERIAL
EXAMINATION SECTION
TEST 1

DIRECTIONS: Each of Questions 1 through 5 consists of a sentence which may or may not be an example of good formal English usage. Examine each sentence, considering grammar, punctuation, spelling, capitalization, and awkwardness. Then choose the correct statement about it from the four options below it. If the English usage in the sentence given is better than any of the changes suggested in options B, C, or D, pick option A. (Do not pick an option that will change the meaning of the sentence.) *PRINT THE LETTER OF THE CORRECT ANSWER IN THE SPACE AT THE RIGHT.*

1. I don't know who could possibly of broken it. 1.____
   A. This is an example of good formal English usage.
   B. The word "who" should be replaced by the word "whom."
   C. The word "of" should be replaced by the word "have."
   D. The word "broken" should be replaced by the word "broke."

2. Telephoning is easier than to write. 2.____
   A. This is an example of good formal English usage.
   B. The word "telephoning" should be spelled "telephoneing."
   C. The word "than" should be replaced by the word "then."
   D. The words "to write" should be replaced by the word "writing."

3. The two operators who have been assigned to these consoles are on vacation. 3.____
   A. This is an example of good formal English usage.
   B. A comma should be placed after the word "operators."
   C. The word "who" should be replaced by the word "whom."
   D. The word "are" should be replaced by the word "is."

4. You were suppose to teach me how to operate a plugboard. 4.____
   A. This is an example of good formal English usage.
   B. The word "were" should be replaced by the word "was."
   C. The word "suppose" should be replaced by the word "supposed."
   D. The word "teach" should be replaced by the word "learn."

5. If you had taken my advice; you would have spoken with him. 5.____
   A. This is an example of good formal English usage.
   B. The word "advice" should be spelled "advise."
   C. The words "had taken" should be replaced by the word "take."
   D. The semicolon should be changed to a comma.

2 (#1)
KEY (CORRECT ANSWERS)

1. C
2. D
3. A
4. C
5. D

TEST 2

DIRECTIONS: Select the correct answer. *PRINT THE LETTER OF THE CORRECT ANSWER IN THE SPACE AT THE RIGHT.*

1. The one of the following sentences which is MOST acceptable from the viewpoint of correct grammatical usage is: 1.____
   A. I do not know which action will have worser results.
   B. He should of known better.
   C. Both the officer on the scene, and his immediate supervisor, is charged with the responsibility.
   D. An officer must have initiative because his supervisor will not always be available to answer questions.

2. The one of the following sentences which is MOST acceptable from the viewpoint of correct grammatical usage is: 2.____
   A. Of all the officers available, the better one for the job will be picked.
   B. Strict orders were given to all the officers, except he.
   C. Study of the law will enable you to perform your duties more efficiently.
   D. It seems to me that you was wrong in failing to search the two men.

3. The one of the following sentences which does NOT contain a misspelled word is: 3.____
   A. The duties you will perform are similar to the duties of a patrolman.
   B. Officers must be constantly alert to sieze the initiative.
   C. Officers in this organization are not entitled to special privileges.
   D. Any changes in procedure will be announced publically.

4. The one of the following sentences which does NOT contain a misspelled word is: 4.____
   A. It will be to your advantage to keep your firearm in good working condition.
   B. There are approximately fourty men on sick leave.
   C. Your first duty will be to pursuade the person to obey the law.
   D. Fires often begin in flameable material kept in lockers.

5. The one of the following sentences which does NOT contain a misspelled word is: 5.____
   A. Offices are not required to perform technical maintainance.
   B. He violated the regulations on two occasions.
   C. Every employee will be held responable for errors.
   D. This was his nineth absence in a year.

KEY (CORRECT ANSWERS)

1. D
2. C
3. C
4. A
5. B

TEST 3

DIRECTIONS: Select the correct answer. *PRINT THE LETTER OF THE CORRECT ANSWER IN THE SPACE AT THE RIGHT.*

1. You are answering a letter that was written on the letterhead of the ABC Company and signed by James H. Wood, Treasurer.
What is usually considered to be the correct salutation to use in your reply?
    A. Dear ABC Company:
    B. Dear Sirs:
    C. Dear Mr. Wood:
    D. Dear Mr. Treasurer:

    1.____

2. Assume that one of your duties is to handle routine letters of inquiry from the public.
The one of the following which is usually considered to be MOST desirable in replying to such a letter is a
    A. detailed answer handwritten on the original letter of inquiry
    B. phone call, since you can cover details more easily over the phone than in a letter
    C. short letter giving the specific information requested
    D. long letter discussing all possible aspects of the question raised

    2.____

3. The CHIEF reason for dividing a letter into paragraphs is to
    A. make the message clear to the reader by starting a new paragraph for each new topic
    B. make a short letter occupy as much of the page as possible
    C. keep the reader's attention by providing a pause from time to time
    D. make the letter look neat and businesslike

    3.____

4. Your superior has asked you to send an e-mail from your agency to a government agency in another city. He has written out the message and has indicated the name of the government agency.
When you dictate the message to your secretary, which of the following items that your superior has NOT mentioned must you be sure to include?
    A. Today's date
    B. The full address of the government agency
    C. A polite opening such as "Dear Sirs"
    D. A final sentence such as "We would appreciate hearing from your agency in reply as soon as is convenient for you"

    4.____

5. The one of the following sentences which is grammatically preferable to the others is:
    A. Our engineers will go over your blueprints so that you may have no problems in construction.
    B. For a long time he had been arguing that we, not he, are to blame for the confusion.
    C. I worked on this automobile for two hours and still cannot find out what is wrong with it.
    D. Accustomed to all kinds of hardships, fatigue seldom bothers veteran policemen.

    5.____

KEY (CORRECT ANSWERS)

1. C
2. C
3. A
4. B
5. A

TEST 4

DIRECTIONS: Select the correct answer. *PRINT THE LETTER OF THE CORRECT ANSWER IN THE SPACE AT THE RIGHT.*

1. Suppose that an applicant for a job as snow laborer presents a letter from a former employer stating: "John Smith has a pleasing manner and never got into an argument with his fellow employees. He was never late or absent."
   This letter
   A. indicates that with some training Smith will make a good snow gang boss
   B. presents no definite evidence of Smith's ability to do snow work
   C. proves definitely that Smith has never done any snow work before
   D. proves definitely that Smith will do better than average work as a snow laborer

   1.____

2. Suppose you must write a letter to a local organization in your section refusing a request in connection with collection of their refuse.
   You should start the letter by
   A. explaining in detail the consideration you gave the request
   B. praising the organization for its service to the community
   C. quoting the regulation which forbids granting the request
   D. stating your regret that the request cannot be granted

   2.____

3. Suppose a citizen writes in for information as to whether or not he may sweep refuse into the gutter. A Sanitation officer answers as follows:
   Dear Sir:
     No person is permitted to litter, sweep, throw or cast, or direct, suffer or permit any person under his control to litter, sweep, throw or cast any ashes, garbage, paper, dust, or other rubbish or refuse into any public street or place, vacant lot, air shaft, areaway, backyard or court.
               Very truly yours,
               John Doe
   This letter is *poorly* written CHIEFLY because
   A. the opening is not indented   B. the thought is not clear
   C. the tone is too formal and cold   D. there are too many commas used

   3.____

4. A section of a disciplinary report written by a Sanitation officer states: "It is requested that subject Sanitation man be advised that his future activities be directed towards reducing his recurrent tardiness else disciplinary action will be initiated which may result in summary discharge."
   This section of the report is *poorly* written MAINLY because
   A. at least one word is misspelled   B. it is not simply expressed
   C. more than one idea is expressed   D. the purpose is not stated

   4.____

5. A section of a disciplinary report written by an officer states: "He comes in late. He takes too much time for lunch. He is lazy. I recommend his services be dispensed with."
   This section of the report is *poorly* written MAINLY because
   A. it ends with a preposition   B. it is not well organized
   C. no supporting facts are stated   D. the sentences are too simple

   5.____

KEY (CORRECT ANSWERS)

1. B
2. D
3. C
4. B
5. C

WRITTEN ENGLISH EXPRESSION
EXAMINATION SECTION
TEST 1

Questions 1-5.

DIRECTIONS: Each of the following sentences may be classified under one of the following four categories:
- A. faulty because of incorrect grammar
- B. faulty because of incorrect punctuation
- C. faulty because of incorrect capitalization or incorrect spelling
- D. correct

Examine each sentence carefully. Then, in the space at the right, print the letter preceding the option which is BEST of those suggested above. All incorrect sentences contain but one type of error. Consider a sentence correct if it contains none of the types of errors mentioned, even though there may be other correct ways of expressing the same thought.

1. They told both he and I that the prisoner had escaped. 1.____

2. Any superior officer, who, disregards the just complaints of his subordinates, is remiss in the performance of his duty. 2.____

3. Only those members of the national organization who resided in the Middle West attended the conference in Chicago. 3.____

4. We told him to give the investigation assignment to whoever was available. 4.____

5. Please do not disappoint and embarrass us by not appearing in court. 5.____

Questions 6-10.

DIRECTIONS: Each of the following sentences may be classified under one of the following four categories:
- A. faulty because of incorrect spelling only
- B. faulty because of incorrect grammar or word usage only
- C. faulty because of one error in spelling and one error in grammar or word usage
- D. correct

Examine each sentence carefully. Then, in the space at the right, print the letter preceding the option which is BEST of those suggested above. All incorrect sentences contain but one type of error. Consider a sentence correct if it contains none of the types of errors mentioned, even though there may be other correct ways of expressing the same thought.

6. Although the officer's speech proved to be entertaining, the topic was not relevant to the main theme of the conference.   6._____

7. In February all new officers attended a training course in which they were learned their principal duties and the fundamental operating procedures of the department.   7._____

8. I personally seen inmate Jones threaten inmates Smith and Green with bodily harm if they refused to participate in the plot.   8._____

9. To the layman, who on a chance visit to the prison observes everything functioning smoothly, the maintenance of prison discipline may seem to be a relatively easily realizable objective.   9._____

10. The prisoners in cell block fourty were forbidden to lay on the cell cots during the recreation hour.   10._____

Questions 11-22.

DIRECTIONS: Each of the following sentences may be classified under one of the following four categories:
A. faulty because of incorrect grammar
B. faulty because of incorrect punctuation
C. faulty because of incorrect capitalization or incorrect spelling
D. correct

Examine each sentence carefully. Then, in the space at the right, print the letter preceding the option which is BEST of those suggested above. All incorrect sentences contain but one type of error. Consider a sentence correct if it contains none of the types of errors mentioned, even though there may be other correct ways of expressing the same thought.

11. I cannot encourage you any.   11._____

12. You always look well in those sort of clothes.   12._____

13. Shall we go to the park?   13._____

14. The man whome he introduced was Mr. Carey.   14._____

15. She saw the letter laying here this morning.   15._____

16. It should rain before the Afternoon is over.   16._____

17. They have already went home.   17._____

18. That Jackson will be elected is evident.   18._____

19. He does not hardly approve of us.   19._____

3 (#1)

20. It was he, who won the prize. 20.____

21. Shall we go to the park. 21.____

22. They are, alike, in this particular. 22.____

KEY (CORRECT ANSWERS)

1.	A	11.	A
2.	B	12.	A
3.	C	13.	D
4.	D	14.	C
5.	C	15.	A
6.	A	16.	C
7.	C	17.	A
8.	B	18.	D
9.	D	19.	A
10.	C	20.	B

21. B
22. B

TEST 2

DIRECTIONS: Among the sentences in this test are some which cannot be accepted inn formal, written English for one or another of the following reasons:

POOR DICTION: The use of a word which is improper either because its meaning does not fit the sentence or because it is not acceptable in formal writing.
Example: The audience was strongly effected by the senator's speech.

VERBOSITY: Repetitious elements adding nothing to the meaning of the sentence and not justified by any need for special emphasis.
Example: At that time there was then no right of petition.

FAULTY GRAMMAR: Word forms and expressions which do not conform to the grammatical and structural usages required by formal written English (errors in case, number, parallelisms, and the like).
Example: Everyone in the delegation had their reasons for opposing the measure.

No sentence has more than one kind of error. Some sentences have no errors. Read each sentence carefully; then, in the space at the right, print the letter:
- D, if the sentence contains an error in diction
- V, if the sentence is verbose
- G, if the sentence contains faulty grammar
- O, if the sentence contains none of these errors

1. I will not go unless I receive a special invitation.

2. The pilot shouted decisive orders to his assistant as the plane burst into flames.

3. She acts like her feelings were hurt.

4. Please come here and try and help me finish this piece of work.

5. As long as you are ready, you may as well start promptly and on time.

6. My younger brother insists that he is as tall as me.

7. A spiritual person is usually deeply concerned with mundane affairs.

8. Speaking from practical experience, I advise you to give up those unquestionably quixotic schemes.

9. We walked as long as there was any light to guide us.

10. Realizing I had forgotten my gloves, I returned to the theatre, using a flashlight and turned down every seat.

11. The winters were hard and dreary, nothing could live without shelter.

2 (#2)

12. Not one in a thousand readers take the matter seriously.   12._____

13. This tire has so many defections that it is worthless.   13._____

14. The jury were divided in their views.   14._____

15. He was so credulous that his friends found it hard to deceive him.   15._____

16. The emperor's latest ukase is sure to stir up such resentment that the people will revolt.   16._____

17. When you go to the library tomorrow, please bring this book to the librarian in the reference room.   17._____

18. His speech is so precise as to seem infected.   18._____

19. I had sooner serve overseas before I remain inactive at home.   19._____

20. We read each others' letters together.   20._____

KEY (CORRECT ANSWERS)

1. O
2. V Eliminate decisive
3. G Use *as though* instead of like
4. V Eliminate and try
5. V Eliminate and on time
6. G *I* instead of me
7. D Mundane means worldly; what is needed here is *religious* or *ethereal*
8. O
9. O
10. G To achieve parallelism and balance, rewrite as follows: "...*and, using a flashlight, turned down every seat.*"
11. G Semicolon (;) after dreary instead of comma (,)
12. G *Takes*, not take
13. D *Defects*, not defections
14. O
15. D *Easy*, not hard
16. O
17. D *Take*, not bring
18. D *Affected*, not infected
19. G Replace before I by *than*
20. V Eliminate *together*

159

TEST 3

DIRECTIONS: Among the sentences in this test are some which cannot be accepted inn formal, written English for one or another of the following reasons:

POOR DICTION: The use of a word which is improper either because its meaning does not fit the sentence or because it is not acceptable in formal writing.
Example: The audience was strongly effected by the senator's speech.

VERBOSITY: Repetitious elements adding nothing to the meaning of the sentence and not justified by any need for special emphasis.
Example: At that time there was then no right of petition.

FAULTY GRAMMAR: Word forms and expressions which do not conform to the grammatical and structural usages required by formal written English (errors in case, number, parallelisms, and the like).
Example: Everyone in the delegation had their reasons for opposing the measure.

No sentence has more than one kind of error. Some sentences have no errors. Read each sentence carefully; then, in the space at the right, print the letter:
    D, if the sentence contains an error in diction
    V, if the sentence is verbose
    G, if the sentence contains faulty grammar
    O, if the sentence contains none of these errors

1. Choose an author as you choose a friend.   1.____

2. Home is home, be it ever so humble and so plain.   2.____

3. Invidious smokers usually find it difficult to break the habit.   3.____

4. You always look devastating in that sort of clothes.   4.____

5. We had no sooner entered the room when the bell rang.   5.____

6. A box of choice figs was sent him for Christmas.   6.____

7. Neither Charles or his brother finished his assignment.   7.____

8. There goes the last piece of cake and the last spoonful of ice cream.   8.____

9. Diamonds are more desired than any precious stones.   9.____

10. The administrator's unconscionable demands elated the workers.   10.____

11. Never before, to the best of my recollection, has there been such promising students.   11.____

2 (#3)

12. It is only because your manners are so objectionable that you are not invited to the party.   12.____

13. An altruistic proverb is: "God helps those who help themselves."   13.____

14. I fully expected that the children would be at their desks and to find them ready to begin work.   14.____

15. A complete system of railroads covers and crisscrosses the entire country.   15.____

16. Our vacation being over, I am sorry to say.   16.____

17. It is so dark that I can't hardly see.   17.____

18. Either you or I am right; we cannot both be right.   18.____

19. After it had laid in the rain all night, it was not fit for use again.   19.____

20. Although the meaning was implicit, the statement required further explanation.   20.____

KEY (CORRECT ANSWERS)

1. O
2. V   Eliminate and so plain
3. D   *Inveterate*, not invidious
4. D   *Well*, not devastating
5. G   *Than*, for well
6. O
7. G   *Nor*, for or
8. G   *Go*, for goes
9. G   Insert *other* after any
10. D   *Embittered*, not elated
11. G   *Have*, not has
12. O
13. D   Not altruistic, *selfish*
14. G   To assure parallelism and balance, place comma (,) after desks, and eliminate and to find them
15. V   Eliminate and crisscrosses
16. G   Replace being by *is*
17. G   *Can hardly see*, not can't hardly see
18. O
19. D,G   *Lain*, not laid
20. O

TEST 4

DIRECTIONS: Among the sentences in this test are some which cannot be accepted inn formal, written English for one or another of the following reasons:

POOR DICTION: The use of a word which is improper either because its meaning does not fit the sentence or because it is not acceptable in formal writing.
Example: The audience was strongly effected by the senator's speech.

VERBOSITY: Repetitious elements adding nothing to the meaning of the sentence and not justified by any need for special emphasis.
Example: At that time there was then no right of petition.

FAULTY GRAMMAR: Word forms and expressions which do not conform to the grammatical and structural usages required by formal written English (errors in case, number, parallelisms, and the like).
Example: Everyone in the delegation had their reasons for opposing the measure.

No sentence has more than one kind of error. Some sentences have no errors. Read each sentence carefully; then, in the space at the right, print the letter:
    D, if the sentence contains an error in diction
    V, if the sentence is verbose
    G, if the sentence contains faulty grammar
    O, if the sentence contains none of these errors

1. Neither Tom nor John were present for the rehearsal.   1._____

2. She admired the cavalier manner with which her husband treated her.   2._____

3. The happiness or misery of men's lives depend on their early training.   3._____

4. Honor as well as profit are to be gained by those studies.   4._____

5. The egg business is only incidental to the regular business of the general store.   5._____

6. It was superior in every way to the book previously read.   6._____

7. We found his captious suggestions to be friendly and constructive.   7._____

8. His testimony today is completely and radically different from that of yesterday.   8._____

9. If you would have studied the problem carefully you would have found the solution more quickly.   9._____

10. The large tips he received made the job a highly lucid one despite its long hours.   10._____

11. The flowers smelled so sweet that the whole house was perfumed.   11._____

2 (#4)

12. When either or both habits becomes fixed, the student improves.   12._____

13. Neither his words nor his action were justifiable.   13._____

14. A calm almost always comes before a storm.   14._____

15. The gallery with all its pictures were destroyed.   15._____

16. Those trees which are not deciduous remain green and attractive all winter.   16._____

17. Whom did they say won?   17._____

18. The man whom I thought was my friend deceived me.   18._____

19. Send whoever will do the work.   19._____

20. The question of who should be the leader arose and the power he should have.   20._____

KEY (CORRECT ANSWERS)

1. G *Was*, not <u>were</u>
2. D *Resented* for <u>admired</u>
3. G *Depends* for <u>depend</u>
4. G *Is* for <u>are</u>
5. O
6. O
7. D *Careful*, not <u>captious</u>
8. V Eliminate <u>completely and radically</u>
9. G *Had you studied…* is to be submitted for <u>If you would have studied</u>
10. D *Lucrative*, not <u>lucid</u>
11. O
12. G *Become*, not <u>becomes</u>
13. G Use *was* instead of <u>were</u>
14. O
15. G *Was destroyed*, not <u>were destroyed</u>
16. O
17. G *Who*, not <u>whom</u>
18. G *Who*, not <u>whom</u>
19. O
20. G Attain parallelism by placing <u>arose</u> at the end of this sentence

TEST 5

DIRECTIONS: Among the sentences in this test are some which cannot be accepted inn formal, written English for one or another of the following reasons:

POOR DICTION: The use of a word which is improper either because its meaning does not fit the sentence or because it is not acceptable in formal writing.
Example: The audience was strongly effected by the senator's speech.

VERBOSITY: Repetitious elements adding nothing to the meaning of the sentence and not justified by any need for special emphasis.
Example: At that time there was then no right of petition.

FAULTY GRAMMAR: Word forms and expressions which do not conform to the grammatical and structural usages required by formal written English (errors in case, number, parallelisms, and the like).
Example: Everyone in the delegation had their reasons for opposing the measure.

No sentence has more than one kind of error. Some sentences have no errors. Read each sentence carefully; then, in the space at the right, print the letter:
- D, if the sentence contains an error in diction
- V, if the sentence is verbose
- G, if the sentence contains faulty grammar
- O, if the sentence contains none of these errors

1. The town consists of three distinct sections, of which the western one is by far the larger. 1.____

2. Of London and Paris, the former is the wealthiest. 2.____

3. The omniscient clap of thunder was not followed by a storm. 3.____

4. Chicago is larger than any city in Illinois. 4.____

5. America is the greatest nation, and of all other nations England is the greater. 5.____

6. Amalgamating their forces helped the two generals to defeat the enemy. 6.____

7. There are very good and sufficient grounds for such a decision. 7.____

8. Due to bad weather, the game was postponed. 8.____

9. The door opens, and in walks John and Mary. 9.____

10. Where but America is there greater prosperity? 10.____

11. The coffee grounds left a sedentary deposit in the cup. 11.____

12. I can but do my best. 12._____
13. I cannot help but comparing him with his predecessor. 13._____
14. Many of Aesop's Fables are parodies from which we can profit. 14._____
15. I wish that I was in Florida now. 15._____
16. I like this kind of grapes better than any other. 16._____
17. The remainder of the time was spent in prayer. 17._____
18. Immigration is when people come into a foreign country to live. 18._____
19. He coughed continuously last winter. 19._____
20. The method is different than the one that was formerly used. 20._____

KEY (CORRECT ANSWERS)

1. G *Largest* for larger
2. G *Wealthier* for wealthiest
3. D *Ominous*, not omniscient
4. G Insert *other* before city
5. G *Greatest* should replace greater at the end of this sentence
6. O
7. V Eliminate and sufficient
8. G *Because of*, not due to
9. G *Walk*, not walks
10. G Insert *in* before America
11. D *Sedimentary*, not sedentary
12. O
13. G Eliminate but
14. D *Parables* not parodies
15. G *Were*, not was
16. O
17. O
18. G Rewrite: *Immigration denotes people coming into…*
19. D *Continually*, not continuously
20. G *From*, not than

WRITTEN ENGLISH EXPRESSION
EXAMINATION SECTION
TEST 1

DIRECTIONS: In each of the following groups of sentences, one of the four sentences is faulty in grammar, punctuation, or capitalization. Select the INCORRECT sentence in each case. *PRINT THE LETTER OF THE CORRECT ANSWER IN THE SPACE AT THE RIGHT.*

1.
   A. If you had stood at home and done your homework, you would not have failed in arithmetic.
   B. Her affected manner annoyed every member of the audience.
   C. How will the new law affect our income taxes?
   D. The plants were not affected by the long, cold winter, but they succumbed to the drought of summer.

   1.____

2.
   A. He is one of the most able men who have been in the Senate.
   B. It is he who is to blame for the lamentable mistake.
   C. Haven't you a helpful suggestion to make at this time?
   D. The money was robbed from the blind man's cup.

   2.____

3.
   A. The amount of children in this school is steadily increasing.
   B. After taking an apple from the table, she went out to play.
   C. He borrowed a dollar from me.
   D. I had hoped my brother would arrive before me.

   3.____

4.
   A. Whom do you think I hear from every week?
   B. Who do you think is the right man for the job?
   C. Who do you think I found in the room?
   D. He is the man whom we considered a good candidate for the presidency.

   4.____

5.
   A. Quietly the puppy laid down before the fireplace.
   B. You have made your bed; now lie in it.
   C. I was badly sunburned because I had lain too long in the sun.
   D. I laid the doll on the bed and left the room.

   5.____

6.
   A. Sailing down the bay was a thrilling experience for me.
   B. He was not consulted about your joining the club.
   C. This story is different than the one I told you yesterday.
   D. There is no doubt about his being the best player.

   6.____

7. A. He maintains there is but one road to world peace.
   B. It is common knowledge that a child sees much he is not supposed to see.
   C. Much of the bitterness might have been avoided if arbitration had been restored to earlier in the meeting.
   D. The man decided it would be advisable to marry a girl somewhat younger than him.

   7.____

8. A. In this book, the incident I liked least is where the hero tries to put out the forest fire.
   B. Learning a foreign language will undoubtedly give a person a better understanding of his mother tongue.
   C. His actions made us wonder what he planned to do next.
   D. Because of the war, we were unable to travel during the summer vacation.

   8.____

9. A. The class had no sooner become interested in the lesson than the dismissal bell rang.
   B. There is little agreement about the kind of world to be planned at the peace conference.
   C. "Today," said the teacher, "we shall read 'The Wind in the Willows.' I am sure you'll like it."
   D. The terms of the legal settlement of the family quarrel handicapped both sides for many years.

   9.____

10. A. I was so surprised that I was not able to say a word.
    B. She is taller than any other member of the class.
    C. It would be much more preferable if you were never seen in his company.
    D. We had no choice but to excuse her for being late.

    10.____

KEY (CORRECT ANSWERS)

1.	A	6.	C
2.	D	7.	D
3.	A	8.	A
4.	C	9.	C
5.	A	10.	C

TEST 2

DIRECTIONS: In each of the following groups of sentences, one of the four sentences is faulty in grammar, punctuation, or capitalization. Select the INCORRECT sentence in each case. *PRINT THE LETTER OF THE CORRECT ANSWER IN THE SPACE AT THE RIGHT.*

1. A. Please send me these data at the earliest opportunity. 1.____
   B. The loss of their material proved to be a severe handicap.
   C. My principal objection to this plan is that it is impracticable.
   D. The doll had laid in the rain for an hour and was ruined.

2. A. The garden scissors, left out all night in the rain, were in a badly rusted condition. 2.____
   B. The girls felt bad about the misunderstanding which had arisen.
   C. Sitting near the campfire, the old man told John and I about many exciting adventures he had had.
   D. Neither of us is in a position to undertake a task of that magnitude.

3. A. The general concluded that one of the three roads would lead to the besieged city. 3.____
   B. The children didn't, as a rule, do hardly anything beyond what they were told to do.
   C. The reason the girl gave for her negligence was that she had acted on the spur of the moment.
   D. The daffodils and tulips look beautiful in that blue vase.

4. A. If I was ten years older, I should be interested in this work. 4.____
   B. Give the prize to whoever has drawn the best picture.
   C. When you have finished reading the book, take it back to the library.
   D. My drawing is as good as or better than yours.

5. A. He asked me whether the substance was animal or vegetable. 5.____
   B. An apple which is unripe should not be eaten by a child.
   C. That was an insult to me who am your friend.
   D. Some spy must of reported the matter to the enemy.

6. A. Limited time makes quoting the entire message impossible. 6.____
   B. Who did she say was going?
   C. The girls in your class have dressed more dolls this year than we.
   D. There was such a large amount of books on the floor that I couldn't find a place for my rocking chair.

7. A. What with his sleeplessness and his ill health, he was unable to assume any responsibility for the success of the meeting. 7.____
   B. If I had been born in February, I should be celebrating my birthday soon.
   C. In order to prevent breakage, she placed a sheet of paper between each of the plates when she packed them.
   D. After the spring shower, the violets smelled very sweet.

8. A. He had laid the book down very reluctantly before the end of the lesson.
   B. The dog, I am sorry to say, had lain on the bed all night.
   C. The cloth was first lain on a flat surface; then it was pressed with a hot iron.
   D. While we were in Florida, we lay in the sun until we were noticeably tanned.

   8.____

9. A. If John was in New York during the recent holiday season, I have no doubt he spent most of time with his parents.
   B. How could he enjoy the television program; the dog was barking and the baby was crying.
   C. When the problem was explained to the class, he must have been asleep.
   D. She wished that her new dress were finished so that she could go to the party.

   9.____

10. A. The engine not only furnishes power but light and heat as well.
    B. You're aware that we've forgotten whose guilt was established, aren't you?
    C. Everybody knows that the woman made many sacrifices for her children.
    D. A man with his dog and gun is a familiar sight in this neighborhood.

    10.____

KEY (CORRECT ANSWERS)

1.	D	6.	D
2.	C	7.	B
3.	B	8.	C
4.	A	9.	B
5.	D	10.	A

TEST 3

DIRECTIONS: Each of sentences 1 through 18 may be classified most appropriately under one of the following three categories:
- A. faulty because of incorrect grammar
- B. faulty because of incorrect punctuation
- C. correct

Examine each sentence carefully. Then, in the space at the right, print the capital letter preceding the option which is BEST of the three suggested above. All incorrect sentences contain but one type of error. Consider a sentence correct if it contains none of the types of errors mentioned, even though there may be other correct ways of expressing the same thought.

1. He sent the notice to the clerk who you hired yesterday.   1.____

2. It must be admitted, however that you were not informed of this change.   2.____

3. Only the employees who have served in this grade for at least two years are eligible for promotion.   3.____

4. The work was divided equally between she and Mary.   4.____

5. He thought that you were not available at that time.   5.____

6. When the messenger returns; please give him this package.   6.____

7. The new secretary prepared, typed, addressed, and delivered, the notices.   7.____

8. Walking into the room, his desk can be seen at the rear.   8.____

9. Although John has worked here longer than she, he produces a smaller amount of work.   9.____

10. She said she could of typed this report yesterday.   10.____

11. Neither one of these procedures are adequate for the efficient performance of this task.   11.____

12. The typewriter is the tool of the typist; the cash register, the tool of the cashier.   12.____

13. "The assignment must be completed as soon as possible" said the supervisor.   13.____

14. As you know, office handbooks are issued to all new employees.   14.____

15. Writing a speech is sometimes easier than to deliver it before an audience.   15.____

16. Mr. Brown, our accountant, will audit the accounts next week. 16.____

17. Give the assignment to whomever is able to do it most efficiently. 17.____

18. The supervisor expected either your or I to file these reports. 18.____

KEY (CORRECT ANSWERS)

1.	A	11.	A
2.	B	12.	C
3.	C	13.	B
4.	A	14.	C
5.	C	15.	A
6.	B	16.	B
7.	B	17.	A
8.	A	18.	A
9.	C		
10.	A		

TEST 4

DIRECTIONS: Each sentence may be classified most appropriately under one of the following four categories:
- A. faulty because of incorrect grammar
- B. faulty because of incorrect punctuation
- C. faulty because of incorrect spelling
- D. correct

Examine each sentence carefully. Then, in the space at the right, print the capital letter preceding the BEST of the four suggested above. All incorrect sentences contain but one type of error. Consider a sentence correct if it contains none of the types of errors mentioned, even though there may be other correct ways of expressing the same thought.

1. The fire apparently started in the storeroom, which is usually locked. 1.____
2. On approaching the victim two bruises were noticed by this officer. 2.____
3. The officer, who was there examined the report with great care. 3.____
4. Each employee in the office had a seperate desk. 4.____
5. All employees including members of the clerical staff, were invited to the lecture. 5.____
6. The suggested procedure is similar to the one now in use. 6.____
7. No one was more pleased with the new procedure than the chauffeur. 7.____
8. He tried to pursuade her to change the procedure. 8.____
9. The total of the expenses charged to petty cash were high. 9.____
10. An understanding between him and I was finally reached. 10.____

KEY (CORRECT ANSWERS)

1. D
2. A
3. B
4. C
5. B
6. D
7. D
8. C
9. A
10. A

TEST 5

Questions 1-5.

DIRECTIONS: Each of sentences 1 to 5 may be classified under one of the following four categories:
- A. faulty because of incorrect grammar
- B. faulty because of incorrect punctuation
- C. faulty because of incorrect capitalization or incorrect spelling
- D. correct

Examine each sentence carefully to determine under which of the above four options it is best classified. Then, in the space at the right, print the capital letter preceding the option which is the BEST of the four suggested above. Each faulty sentence contains but one type of error. Consider a sentence to be correct if it contains none of the types of errors mentioned, even though there may be other correct ways of expressing the same thought.

1. They told both he and I that the prisoner had escaped. 1.____

2. Any superior officer, who, disregards the just complaints of his subordinates, is remiss in the performance of his duty. 2.____

3. Only those members of the National organization who resided in the Middle West attended the conference in Chicago. 3.____

4. We told him to give the investigation assignment to whoever was available. 4.____

5. Please do not disappoint and embarass us by not appearing in court. 5.____

Questions 6-10.

DIRECTIONS: Each of questions 6 through 10 consists of a sentence. Read each sentence carefully and then write your answer to each question according to the following scheme:
- A. Sentence contains an error in spelling only
- B. Sentence contains an error in grammar or word usage only
- C. Sentence contains one error in spelling and one error in grammar or word usage
- D. Sentence is correct; contains no errors

6. Although the officer's speech proved to be entertaining, the topic was not relevant to the main theme of the conference. 6.____

7. In February all new officers attended a training course in which they were learned their principal duties and the fundamental operating procedures of the department. 7.____

2 (#5)

8. I personally seen inmate Jones threaten inmates Smith and Green with bodily 8.____
harm if they refused to participate in the plot.

9. To the layman, who on a chance visit to the prison observes everything 9.____
functioning smoothly, the maintenance of prison discipline may seem to be a
relatively easily realizable objective.

10. The prisoners in cell block fourty were forbidden to lay on the cell cots during 10.____
the recreation hour.

KEY (CORRECT ANSWERS)

1. A   6. D
2. B   7. C
3. C   8. B
4. D   9. D
5. C   10. C

TEST 6

DIRECTIONS: Each of the following sentences may be classified under one of the following four categories:
   A. faulty because of incorrect grammar
   B. faulty because of incorrect punctuation
   C. faulty because of incorrect capitalization or incorrect spelling
   D. correct

Examine each sentence carefully to determine under which of the above four options it is best classified. Then, in the space at the right, print the capital letter preceding the option which is the BEST of the four suggested above. Each faulty sentence contains but one type of error. Consider a sentence to be correct if it contains none of the types of errors mentioned, even though there may be other correct ways of expressing the same thought.

1. I cannot encourage you any.   1.____
2. You always look well in those sort of clothes.   2.____
3. Shall we go to the park?   3.____
4. The man whome he introduced was Mr. Carey.   4.____
5. She saw the letter laying here this morning.   5.____
6. It should rain before the Afternoon is over.   6.____
7. They have already went home.   7.____
8. That Jackson will be elected is evident.   8.____
9. He does not hardly approve of us.   9.____
10. It was he, who won the prize.   10.____

KEY (CORRECT ANSWERS)

1.	A		6.	C
2.	A		7.	A
3.	D		8.	D
4.	C		9.	A
5.	A		10.	B

TEST 7

DIRECTIONS: Each of the following sentences may be classified under one of the following four categories:
   A. faulty because of incorrect grammar
   B. faulty because of incorrect punctuation
   C. faulty because of incorrect capitalization or incorrect spelling
   D. correct

Examine each sentence carefully to determine under which of the above four options it is best classified. Then, in the space at the right, print the capital letter preceding the option which is the BEST of the four suggested above. Each faulty sentence contains but one type of error. Consider a sentence to be correct if it contains none of the types of errors mentioned, even though there may be other correct ways of expressing the same thought.

1. Shall we go to the park. 1._____
2. They are, alike, in this particular. 2._____
3. They gave the poor man sume food when he knocked on the door. 3._____
4. I regret the loss caused by the error. 4._____
5. The students' will have a new teacher. 5._____
6. They sweared to bring out all the facts. 6._____
7. He decided to open a branch store on 33rd street. 7._____
8. His speed is equal and more than that of a racehorse. 8._____
9. He felt very warm on that Summer day. 9._____
10. He was assisted by his friend, who lives in the next house. 10._____

KEY (CORRECT ANSWERS)

1. B   6. A
2. B   7. C
3. C   8. A
4. D   9. C
5. B   10. D

TEST 8

DIRECTIONS: Each of the following sentences may be classified under one of the following four categories:
- A. faulty because of incorrect grammar
- B. faulty because of incorrect punctuation
- C. faulty because of incorrect capitalization or incorrect spelling
- D. correct

Examine each sentence carefully to determine under which of the above four options it is best classified. Then, in the space at the right, print the capital letter preceding the option which is the BEST of the four suggested above. Each faulty sentence contains but one type of error. Consider a sentence to be correct if it contains none of the types of errors mentioned, even though there may be other correct ways of expressing the same thought.

1. The climate of New York is colder than California. 1.____
2. I shall wait for you on the corner. 2.____
3. Did we see the boy who, we think, is the leader. 3.____
4. Being a modest person, John seldom talks about his invention. 4.____
5. The gang is called the smith street boys. 5.____
6. He seen the man break into the store. 6.____
7. We expected to lay still there for quite a while. 7.____
8. He is considered to be the Leader of his organization. 8.____
9. Although I recieved an invitation, I won't go. 9.____
10. The letter must be here some place. 10.____

KEY (CORRECT ANSWERS)

1.	A	6.	A
2.	D	7.	A
3.	B	8.	C
4.	D	9.	C
5.	C	10.	A

TEST 9

DIRECTIONS: Each of the following sentences may be classified under one of the following four categories:
- A. faulty because of incorrect grammar
- B. faulty because of incorrect punctuation
- C. faulty because of incorrect capitalization or incorrect spelling
- D. correct

Examine each sentence carefully to determine under which of the above four options it is best classified. Then, in the space at the right, print the capital letter preceding the option which is the BEST of the four suggested above. Each faulty sentence contains but one type of error. Consider a sentence to be correct if it contains none of the types of errors mentioned, even though there may be other correct ways of expressing the same thought.

1. I thought it to be he. 1.____
2. We expect to remain here for a long time. 2.____
3. The committee was agreed. 3.____
4. Two-thirds of the building are finished. 4.____
5. The water was froze. 5.____
6. Everyone of the salesmen must supply their own car. 6.____
7. Who is the author of Gone With The Wind? 7.____
8. He marched on and declaring that he would never surrender. 8.____
9. Who shall I say called? 9.____
10. Everyone has left but they. 10.____

KEY (CORRECT ANSWERS)

1.	A	6.	A
2.	D	7.	B
3.	A	8.	A
4.	A	9.	D
5.	A	10.	D

TEST 10

DIRECTIONS: Each of the following sentences may be classified under one of the following four categories:
- A. faulty because of incorrect grammar
- B. faulty because of incorrect punctuation
- C. faulty because of incorrect capitalization or incorrect spelling
- D. correct

Examine each sentence carefully to determine under which of the above four options it is best classified. Then, in the space at the right, print the capital letter preceding the option which is the BEST of the four suggested above. Each faulty sentence contains but one type of error. Consider a sentence to be correct if it contains none of the types of errors mentioned, even though there may be other correct ways of expressing the same thought.

1. Who did we give the order to? 1.____
2. Send your order in immediately. 2.____
3. I believe I paid the Bill. 3.____
4. I have not met but one person. 4.____
5. Why aren't Tom, and Fred, going to the dance? 5.____
6. What reason is there for him not going? 6.____
7. The seige of Malta was a tremendous event. 7.____
8. I was there yesterday I assure you. 8.____
9. Your ukulele is better than mine. 9.____
10. No one was there only Mary. 10.____

KEY (CORRECT ANSWERS)

1. A   6. A
2. D   7. C
3. C   8. B
4. A   9. C
5. B   10. A

ENGLISH GRAMMAR AND USAGE
EXAMINATION SECTION
TEST 1

DIRECTIONS: In the passages that follow, certain words and phrases are underlined and numbered. In each question, you will find alternatives for each underlined part. You are to choose the one that BEST expresses the idea, makes the statement appropriate for standard written English, or is worded MOST consistently with the style and tone of the passage as a whole. Choose the alternative you consider BEST and write the letter in the space at the right. If you think the original version is BEST, choose NO CHANGE. Read each passage through once before you begin to answer the questions that accompany it. You cannot determine most answers without reading several sentences beyond the phrase in question. Be sure that you have read far enough ahead each time you choose an alternative.

Questions 1-14.

DIRECTIONS: Questions 1 through 14 are based on the following passage.

Modern filmmaking <u>had began</u> in Paris in 1895 with the work of the Lumiere brothers.
                    1
Using their <u>invention, the Cinématographe,</u> the Lumières were able to photograph, print,
            2
and project moving pictures onto a screen. Their films showed <u>actual occurrences. A train</u>
                                                                            3
approaching a station, people a factory, workers demolishing a wall.

These early films had neither plot nor sound. But another Frenchman, Georges <u>Méliès,</u>

soon incorporated plot lines <u>into</u> his films. And with his attempts to draw upon the potential of
                              4
film to create fantasy <u>worlds</u>. Méliès also <u>was an early pioneer from</u> special film effects. Edwin
                        5   6
Porter, an American filmmaker, took Méliès emphasis on narrative one step further. Believing

<u>that, continuity of shots</u> was of primary importance in filmmaking, Porter connected
    7
<u>images to present,</u> a sustained action. His GREAT TRAIN ROBBERY of 1903 opened a new
    8
era in film.

<u>Because</u> film was still considered <u>as</u> low entertainment in early twentieth century America,
    9   10
it was on its way to becoming a respected art form. Beginning in 1908, the American director

D.W. Griffith discovered and explored techniques to make film a more expressive medium.

2 (#1)

With his technical contributions, as well as his attempts to develop the intellectual and moral
                                11
potential of film, Griffith helped build a solid foundation for the industry.

    Thirty years after the Lumière brothers' first show, sound had yet been added to the
     12   13
movies. Finally, in 1927, Hollywood produced its first *talkie*, THE JAZZ SINGER. With sound,

modern film coming of age.
                  14

1. A. NO CHANGE   B. begun   1.____
    C. began   D. had some beginnings

2. A. NO CHANGE   B. invention—the Cinématographe   2.____
    C. invention, the Cinématgraphe—   D. invention, the Cinématographe

3. A. NO CHANGE   B. actually occurrences, a   3.____
    C. actually occurrences—a D. actual occurrences: a

4. A. NO CHANGE   B. about   4.____
    C. with   D. to

5. A. NO CHANGE   B. worlds   5.____
    C. worlds' and   D. worlds and

6. A. NO CHANGE   B. pioneered   6.____
    C. pioneered the beginnings of   D. pioneered the early beginnings of

7. A. NO CHANGE   B. that continuity of shots   7.____
    C. that, continuity of shots,   D. that continuity of shots

8. A. NO CHANGE   B. images to present   8.____
    C. that, continuity of shots   D. that continuity of shots

9. A. NO CHANGE   9.____
    B. (Begin new paragraph) in view of the fact that
    C. (Begin new paragraph) Although
    D. Do NOT begin new paragraph) Since

10. A. NO CHANGE   B. as if it were   10.____
    C. like it was   D. OMIT the underlined portion

11. A. NO CHANGE   B. similar to   11.____
    C. similar with   D. like with

3 (#1)

12. A. NO CHANGE
    B. (Begin new paragraph) Consequently, thirty
    C. (Do NOT begin new paragraph) Therefore, thirty
    D. (Do NOT begin new paragraph) As a consequence, thirty

    12.____

13. A. NO CHANGE
    B. (Begin new paragraph) Consequently, thirty
    C. (No NOT begin new paragraph) Therefore, thirty
    D. (Do NOT begin new paragraph As a consequence, thirty

    13.____

14. A. NO CHANGE   B. comes
    C. came   D. had came

    14.____

Questions 15-22.

DIRECTIONS: Questions 15 through 22 are based on the following passage.

One of the most awesome forces in nature is the tsunami, or tidal wave. A

<u>tsunami—the word is Japanese for harbor wave,</u> can generate the destructive power of many
                    15
atomic bombs.

<u>Tsunamis usually</u> appear in a series of four or five waves about fifteen minutes apart.
       16
They begin deep in the ocean, gather remarkable speed as they travel, and cover great

instances. The wave triggered by the explosion of Krakatoa in 1883 circled the world in three

days.

<u>Tsunamis being</u> known to sink large ships at sea, they are most dangerous when they
       17
reach land. Close to shore, an oncoming tsunami is forced <u>upward and skyward,</u> perhaps as
                                                                  18
high as 100 feet. This combination of height and speed accounts for the tsunami's great power.

That *tsunami* is a Japanese word is no accident, <u>due to the fact that</u> no nation
                                                           19
<u>frequently</u> has been so visited by giant waves as Japan. <u>Tsunamis</u> reach that country regularly,
  20   21
and with devastating consequences. One Japanese tsunami flattened several towns in

<u>1896, also killed 27,000 people.</u> The 2011 tsunami caused similar loss of life as well as untold
          22
damage from nuclear radiation.

183

15. A. NO CHANGE
    B. tsunami, the word is Japanese for harbor wave—
    C. tsunami—the word is Japanese for harbor wave—
    D. tsunami—the word being Japanese for harbor wave,

16. A. NO CHANGE
    B. (Begin new paragraph) Consequently, tsunamis
    C. (Do NOT begin new paragraph) Tsunamis consequently
    D. (Do NOT begin new paragraph) Yet, tsunamis

17. A. NO CHANGE
    B. Because tsunamis have been
    C. Although tsunamis have been
    D. Tsunamis have been

18. A. NO CHANGE
    B. upward to the sky,
    C. upward in the sky
    D. upward,

19. A. NO CHANGE
    B. when one takes into consideration the fact that
    C. seeing as how
    D. for

20. A. NO CHANGE
    B. (Place after *has*)
    C. (Place after *so*)
    D. (Place after *visited*)

21. A. NO CHANGE
    B. Moreover, tsunamis
    C. However, tsunamis
    D. Because tsunamis

22. A. NO CHANGE
    B. 1896 and killed 27,000 people
    C. 1896 and killing 27,000 people
    D. 1896, and 27,000 people as well

Questions 23-33.

DIRECTIONS: Questions 23 through 33 are based on the following passage.

I was <u>married one</u> August on a farm in Maine. The <u>ceremony, itself, taking</u> place in an
                23   24
arbor of pine boughs <u>we had built and constructed</u> in the yard next to the house. On the morning
                             25
of the wedding day, we parked the tractors behind the shed, <u>have tied</u> the dogs to an oak tree to
                                                          26
keep them from chasing the guests, and put the cows out to pasture. <u>Thus</u> we had thought of
                                                                           27
everything, it seemed. we had forgotten how interested a cow can be in what is going on

<u>around them.</u> During the ceremony, my sister <u>(who has taken several years of lessons)</u> was to
    28   29
play a flute solo. We were all listening intently when she <u>had began</u> to play. As the first notes
                                                                                           30
reached us, we were surprised to hear a bass line under the flute's treble melody. Looking

5 (#1)

around, the source was quickly discovered. There was Star, my pet Guernsey, her head hanging
                31
over the pasture fence, mooing along with the delicate strains of Bach.

   Star took our laughter as being like a compliment, and we took her contribution that way,
                           32
too. It was a sign of approval—the kind you would find only at a farm wedding.

23. A. NO CHANGE   B. married, one   23.____
    C. married on an   D. married, in an

24. A. NO CHANGE   B. ceremony itself taking   24.____
    C. ceremony itself took   D. ceremony, itself took

25. A. NO CHANGE   25.____
    B. which had been built and constructed
    C. we had built and constructed it
    D. we had built

26. A. NO CHANGE   B. tie   26.____
    C. tied   D. tying

27. A. NO CHANGE   27.____
    B. (Do NOT begin new paragraph) And
    C. (Begin new paragraph) But
    D. (Begin new paragraph (Moreover,

28. A. NO CHANGE   B. around her   28.____
    C. in her own vicinity   D. in their immediate area

29. A. NO CHANGE   29.____
    B. (whom has taken many years of lessons)
    C. (who has been trained in music)
    D. OMIT the underlined portion

30. A. NO CHANGE   B. begun   30.____
    C. began   D. would begin

31. A. NO CHANGE   31.____
    B. the discovery of the source was quick
    C. the discovery of the source was quickly made.
    D. we quickly discovered the source.

32. A. NO CHANGE   A. as   32.____
    C. just as   D. as if

33. A. NO CHANGE
    C. But it was
    B. Yet it was
    D. Being

    33._____

Questions 34-42.

DIRECTIONS: Questions 34 through 42 are based on the following passage,

Riding a bicycle in Great Britain is not the same as riding a bicycle in the United States. Americans bicycling in Britain will find some <u>basic fundamental</u> differences in the rules of the
                                                                                34
road and in the attitudes of motorists.

<u>Probably</u> most difficult for the American cyclist is adjusting <u>with</u> British traffic patterns.
  35   36
<u>Knowing that traffic</u> in Britain moves on the left-hand side of the road, bicycling <u>once</u> there is the
    37   38
mirror image of what it is in the United States.

The problem of adjusting to traffic patterns is somewhat lessened, <u>however</u> by the respect
                                                                      39
with which British motorists treat bicyclists. A cyclist in a traffic circle, for example, is given the same right-of-way <u>with</u> the driver of any other vehicle. However, the cyclist is expected to obey
                       40
the rules of the road. <u>This difference in the American and British attitudes toward bicyclists</u> may
                                                       41
stem from differing attitudes toward the bicycle itself. Whereas Americans frequently view bicycles as <u>toys, but</u> the British treat them primarily as vehicles.
              42

34. A. NO CHANGE
    C. basically fundamental
    B. basic and fundamental
    D. basic

    34._____

35. A. NO CHANGE
    C. Therefore, probably
    B. Even so, probably
    D. As a result, probably

    35._____

36. A. NO CHANGE
    C. on
    B. upon
    D. to

    36._____

37. A. NO CHANGE
    C. Because traffic
    B. Seeing that traffic
    D. Traffic

    37._____

38. A. NO CHANGE
    C. once one is
    B. once you are
    D. OMIT the underlined portion

    38._____

7 (#1)

39. A. NO CHANGE B. also, C. moreover, D. therefore, 39.____

40. A. NO CHANGE B. as C. as if D. as with 40.____

41. A. NO CHANGE
B. difference in the American and British attitudes toward bicyclists
C. difference, in the American and British attitudes toward bicyclists
D. difference in the American, and British, attitudes toward bicyclists
41.____

42. A. NO CHANGE B. toy; C. toys, D. toys; but 42.____

Questions 43-51.

DIRECTIONS: Questions 43 through 51 are based on the following passage.

People have always believed that supernatural powers <u>tend toward some influence on</u> lives for good or for ill. Superstition originated with the idea that individuals <u>could in turn,</u> exert
43
                                                                                                                                44
influence <u>at</u> spirits. Certain superstitions are <u>so deeply embedded</u> in our culture that intelligent
         45   46
people sometimes act in accordance with them.

One common superstitious act is knocking on wood after boasting of good fortune. People once believed that gods inhabited trees and, therefore, were present in the wood used to build houses. Fearing that speaking of good luck within the gods' hearing might anger <u>them, people</u>
                                                                                                                                47
knocked on wood to deafen the gods and avoid their displeasure.

Another superstitious <u>custom and practice</u> is throwing salt over the left shoulder.
                                          48
<u>Considering</u> salt was once considered sacred, people thought that spilling it brought bad
   49
luck. Since right and left represented good and evil, the believers used their right hands, which symbolized good, to throw a pinch of salt over their left shoulders into the eyes of the evil gods.

<u>Because of this</u>, people attempted to avert misfortune.
     50
Without realizing the origin of superstitions, many people exhibit superstitious behavior.

<u>Others avoid</u> walking under ladders and stepping on cracks in sidewalks, without having any
     51
idea why they are doing so.

43. A. NO CHANGE
    C. tend to influence on
    B. can influence
    D. are having some influence on

44. A. NO CHANGE.
    C. could, in turn
    B. could, turning
    D. could, in turn,

45. A. NO CHANGE
    C. toward
    B. of
    D. on

46. A. NO CHANGE
    C. deepest embedded
    B. deepest embedded
    D. embedded deepest

47. A. NO CHANGE
    C. them: some people
    B. them; some people
    D. them, they

48. A. NO CHANGE
    C. traditional custom
    B. Custom
    D. customary habit

49. A. NO CHANGE
    C. Because
    B. Although
    D. Keeping in mind that

50. A. NO CHANGE
    C. Consequently
    B. As a result of this,
    D. In this way,

51. A. NO CHANGE
    C. Avoiding
    B. Often avoiding
    D. They avoid

Questions 52-66.

DIRECTIONS: Questions 52 through 65 are based on the following passage.

In the 1920s, the Y.M.C.A. sponsored one of the first programs <u>in order to promote</u>
                                                                              52
more enlightened public opinion on racial matters; the organization started special university

classes <u>in which</u> young people could study race relations. Among the guest speakers invited to
        53
conduct the sessions, one of the most popular was George Washington Carver, the scientist

from Tuskegee Institute.

As a student, Carver himself had been active in the Y.M.C.A. <u>He shared</u> its evangelical
                                                                      54
and educational philosophy. However, in <u>1923,</u> the Y.M.C.A. arranged <u>Carver's first initial</u>
                                          55   56
speaking tour, the scientist accepted with apprehension. He was to speak at several white

colleges, most of whose students had never seen, let alone heard, an educated black man.

9 (#1)

Although Carver's appearances did sometimes cause occasional controversy, but
                                    57   58
his quiet dedication prevailed, and his humor quickly won over his audiences. Nevertheless, for
                                                                              59
the next decade, Carver toured the Northeast, Midwest, and South under Y.M.C.A.

sponsorship. Speaking at places never before open to blacks. On these tours Carver
     60
befriended thousands of students, many of whom subsequently corresponded with his
                                           61
afterwards. The tours, unfortunately were not without discomfort for Carver. There were
   62   63
the indignities of *Jim Crow* accommodations and racial insults from strangers. As a result,
                                                                                  64
the scientist's enthusiasm never faltered. Avoiding any discussion of the political and social
                                              65
aspects of racial injustice; instead, Carver conducted his whole life as an indirect attack to
                                                                                             66
prejudice. This, as much as his science, is his legacy to humankind.

52. A. NO CHANGE   B. to promote   52._____
    C. for the promoting of what is   D. for the promotion of what are

53. A. NO CHANGE   C. from which   53._____
    C. that   D. by which

54. A. NO CHANGE   B. Sharing.   54._____
    C. Having Shared   D. Because He Shared

55. A. NO CHANGE   B. 1923   55._____
    C. 1923, and   D. 1923, when

56. A. NO CHANGE   B. Carvers' first, initial   56._____
    C. Carvers first initial D. Carver's first

57. A. NO CHANGE   B. sometimes did   57._____
    C. did   D. OMIT the underlined portion

58. A. NO CHANGE   B. controversy and   58._____
    C. controversy   D. controversy, however

59. A. NO CHANGE   B. However, for   59._____
    C. However, from   D. For

60. A. NO CHANGE   B. sponsorship and spoke   60._____
    C. sponsorship; and spoke D. sponsorship, and speaking

61. A. NO CHANGE   B. who
    C. them   D. those   61.____

62. A. NO CHANGE   62.____
    B. later
    C. sometimes later.
    D. OMIT the underlined portion and end the sentence with a period

63. A. NO CHANGE   B. tours, unfortunately, were   63.____
    C. tours unfortunately, were   D. tours, unfortunately, are

64. A. NO CHANGE   B. So   64.____
    C. But   D. Therefore,

65. A. NO CHANGE   B. He avoided discussing   65.____
    C. Having avoided discussing   D. Upon avoiding the discussion of

66. A. NO CHANGE   B. over   66.____
    C. on   D. of

Questions 67-75.

DIRECTIONS: Questions 67 through 75 are based on the following passage.

Shooting rapids is not the only way to experience the thrill of canoeing. An ordinary-
                                                                         67
looking stream, innocent of rocks and white water, can provide adventure, as long as it has

three essential features; a swift current, close banks, and has plenty of twists and turns.
               68   69
A powerful current causes tension, for canoeists know they will have only seconds for
70
executing the maneuvers necessary to prevent crashing into the threes lining the narrow

streams banks. Of course, the narrowness, itself, being crucial in creating the tension. On a
      71   72
broad stream, canoeists can pause frequently, catch their breath, and get their bearings.

However to a narrow stream, where every minute you run the risk of being knocked down by a
         73   74
low-hanging tree limb, they be constantly alert. Yet even the fast current and close banks would

be manageable if the stream were fairly straight. The expenditure of energy required to paddle

furiously, first on one side of the canoe and then on the other, wearies both the nerves as well
                                                                        75
as the body.

11 (#1)

67. A. NO CHANGE
    B. They say that for adventure an
    C. Many finding that an
    D. The old saying that an
    67.____

68. A. NO CHANGE
    B. features
    C. features,
    D. features; these being
    68.____

69. A. NO CHANGE
    B. there must be
    C. with
    D. OMIT the underlined portion
    69.____

70. A. NO CHANGE
    B. Thus, a
    C. Therefore, a
    D. Furthermore, a
    70.____

71. A. NO CHANGE
    B. stream's banks.
    C. streams bank's
    D. banks of the streams
    71.____

72. A. NO CHANGE
    B. narrowness, itself is
    C. narrowness itself is
    D. narrowness in itself being
    72.____

73. A. NO CHANGE
    B. near
    C. on
    D. with
    73.____

74. A. NO CHANGE
    B. the canoer runs
    C. one runs
    D. they run
    74.____

75. A. NO CHANGE
    B. the nerves as well as the body
    C. the nerves, also, as well as the body
    D. not only the body but also the nerves as well
    75.____

KEY (CORRECT ANSWERS)

1.	C	21.	A	41.	A	61.	A
2.	A	22.	B	42.	C	62.	D
3.	D	23.	A	43.	B	63.	B
4.	A	24.	C	44.	C	64.	C
5.	B	25.	D	45.	D	65.	B
6.	B	26.	C	46.	A	66.	C
7.	D	27.	C	47.	A	67.	A
8.	B	28.	B	48.	B	68.	B
9.	C	29.	D	49.	C	69.	D
10.	D	30.	C	50.	D	70.	A
11.	A	31.	D	51.	D	71.	B
12.	A	32.	B	52.	B	72.	C
13.	B	33.	A	53.	A	73.	C
14.	C	34.	D	54.	A	74.	D
15.	C	35.	A	55.	D	75.	B
16.	A	36.	D	56.	D		
17.	C	37.	C	57.	C		
18.	D	38.	D	58.	C		
19.	D	39.	A	59.	D		
20.	C	40.	B	60.	B		

EXAMINATION SECTION

TEST 1

DIRECTIONS: Each question or incomplete statement is followed by several suggested answers or completions. Select the one that BEST answers the question or completes the statement. *PRINT THE LETTER OF THE CORRECT ANSWER IN THE SPACE AT THE RIGHT.*

Questions 1-25. A student has written an article for the high school newspaper, using the skills learned in a stenography and typewriting class in its preparation. In the article which follows, certain words or groups of words are underlined and numbered. The underlined word or group of words may be incorrect because they present an error in grammar, usage, sentence structure, capitalization, diction, or punctuation. For each numbered word or group of words, there is an identically numbered question consisting of four choices based only on the underlined portion. Indicate the BEST choice. <u>Unnecessary changes will be considered incorrect.</u>

TIGERS VIE FOR CITY CHAMPIONSHIP

In their second year of varsity football, the North Shore Tigers have gained a shot at the city championship. Last Saturday in the play-offs, the Tigers defeated the Western High School Cowboys, <u>thus eliminated that team</u> from contention. Most of the credit for the
(1)
team's improvement must go to Joe Harris, the coach. <u>To play as well as they do</u> now,
(2)
the coach must have given the team superior instruction. There is no doubt that,

<u>if a coach is effective, his influence is over</u> many young minds.
(3)
With this major victory behind them, the Tigers can now look forward <u>to meet the</u>
(4)
defending champions, the Revere Minutemen, in the finals.

The win over the Cowboys was <u>due</u> to North Side's supremacy in the air. The Tigers'
(5)
players have the advantages of strength and of <u>being speedy</u>. Our sterling quarterback, Butch
(6)
Carter, a master of the long pass, used <u>these kind of passes</u> to bedevil the boys from Western.
(7)
As a matter of fact, if the Tigers <u>would have used</u> the passing offense earlier in the game, the
(8)
score would have been more one-sided. Butch, by the way, our all-around senior student, has already been tapped for bigger things. Having the highest marks in his class, <u>Barton College</u>

has offered him a scholarship.
         (9)

   The team's defense is another story. During the last few weeks, neither the linebackers nor the safety man have shown sufficient ability to contain their opponents' running game. In
                            (10)
the city final, the defensive unit's failing to complete it's assignments may lead to disaster.
                            (11)
However, the coach said that this unit not only has been cooperative but also the coach raise
                                              (12)
their eagerness to learn. He also said that this team has not and never will give up. This kind
                                                          (13)
of spirit is contagious, therefore I predict that the Tigers will win because I have affection and full
                        (14)   (15)
confidence in the team.

   One of the happy surprises this season is Peter Yisko, our punter. Peter is in the United
                                                                              (16)
States for only two years. When he was in grammar school in the old country, it was not necessary for him to have studied hard. Now, he depends on the football team to help him with
                    (17)
his English. Everybody but the team mascot and I have been pressed into service. Peter was
                         (18
ineligible last year when he learned that he would only obtain half of the credits he had
                              (19)
completed in Europe. Nevertheless, he attended occasional practice sessions, but he soon found out that, if one wants to be a successful player, you must realize that regular practice is
                                                         (20)
required. In fact, if a team is to be successful, it is necessary that everyone be present for all
                                                                              (21)
practice sessions. "The life of a football player," says Peter, "is better than a scholar."
                                                                            (22)
   Facing the Minutemen, the Tigers will meet their most formidable opposition yet. This team is not only gaining a bad reputation but also indulging in illegal practices on the field.
       (23)
They can't hardly object to us being technical about penalties under these circumstances.
     (24)
As far as the Minutemen are concerned, a victory will taste sweet like a victory should.
                                           (25)

1. A. that eliminated that team   B. and they were eliminated   1.____
    C. and eliminated them   D. Correct as is

2. A. To make them play as well as they do
    B. Having played so well
    C. After they played so well
    D. Correct as is

3. A. if coaches are effective; they have influence over
    B. to be effective, a coach influences over
    C. if a coach is effective, he influences
    D. Correct as is

4. A. to meet with   B. to meeting
    C. to a meeting of   D. Correct as is

5. A. because of   B. on account of
    C. motivated by   D. Correct as is

6. A. operating swiftly   B. speed
    C. running speedily   D. Correct as is

7. A. these kinds of pass   B. this kind of passes
    C. this kind of pass   D. Correct as is

8. A. would of used   B. had used
    C. were using   D. Correct as is

9. A. he was offered a scholarship by Barton College.
    B. Barton College offered a scholarship to him.
    C. a scholarship was offered him by Barton College
    D. Correct as is

10. A. had shown   B. were showing
    C. has shown   D. Correct as is

11. A. the defensive unit failing to complete its assignment
    B. the defensive unit's failing to complete its assignment
    C. the defensive unit failing to complete it's assignment
    D. Correct as is

12. A. has been not only cooperative, but also eager to learn
    B. has not only been cooperative, but also shows eagerness to learn
    C. has been not only cooperative, but also they were eager to learn
    D. Correct as is

13. A. has not given up and never will
    B. has not and never would give up
    C. has not given up and never will give up
    D. Correct as is

14. A. .Therefore B. : therefore 14.____
    C. —therefore D. Correct as is

15. A. full confidence and affection for 15.____
    B. affection for and full confidence in
    C. affection and full confidence concerning
    D. Correct as is

16. A. is living B. was living 16.____
    C. has been D. Correct as is

17. A. to study B. to be studying 17.____
    C. to have been studying D. Correct as is

18. A. but the team mascot and me has 18.____
    B. but the team mascot and myself has
    C. but the team mascot and me have
    D. Correct as is

19. A. only learned that he would obtain half 19.____
    B. learned that he would obtain only half
    C. learned that he only would obtain half
    D. Correct as is

20. A. a person B. one 20.____
    C. one D. every

21. A. is B. will be 21.____
    C. shall be D. Correct as is

22. A. to be a scholar B. being a scholar 22.____
    C. that of a scholar D. Correct as is

23. A. not only is gaining a bad reputation 23.____
    B. is gaining not only a bad reputation
    C. is not gaining only a bad reputation
    D. Correct as is

24. A. can hardly object to us being B. can hardly object to our being 24.____
    C. can't hardly object to our being D. Correct as is

25. A victory will taste sweet like it should 25.____
    B. victory will taste sweetly as it should taste
    C. victory will taste sweet as a victory should
    D. Correct as is

Questions 26-30.

DIRECTIONS: Questions 26 through 30 are to be answered on the basis of the instructions and paragraph which follow.

The paragraph which follows is part of report prepared by a buyer for submission to his superior. The paragraph contains 5 underlined groups of words, each one bearing a number which identifies the question relating to it. Each of these groups of words MAY or MAY NOT represent standard written English, suitable for use in a formal report. For each question, decide whether the group of words used in the paragraph which is always choice A is standard written English and should be retained, or whether choice B, C, or D.

On October 23, 2009 the vendor delivered two microscopes to the using agency. When they inspected, one microscope was found to have a defective part. The vendor was
    (26)
notified, and offered to replace the defective part; the using agency, however, requested that the microscope be replaced. The vendor claimed that complete replacement was
    (27)
unnecessary and refused to comply with the agency's demand, having the result that the
    (28)
agency declared that it will pay only for the acceptable microscope. At that point I got involved by the agency's contacting me. The agency requested that I speak to the vendor
    (29)
since I handled the original purchase and have dealed with this vendor before.
    (30)

26. A. When they inspected
    B. Upon inspection
    C. The inspection report said that
    D. Having inspected,

27. A. that the microscope be replaced
    B. a whole new microscope in replacement
    C. to have a replacement for the microscope
    D. that they get the microscope replaced

28. A. , having the result that the agency declared
    B. ; the agency consequently declared
    C. , which refusal caused the agency to consequently declare
    D. , with the result of the agency's declaring

29. A. I got involved by the agency's contacting me
    B. I became involved, being contacted by the agency
    C. the agency contacting me, I got involved
    D. the agency contacted me and I became involved

30. A. have dealed with this vendor before.
    B. done business before with this vendor.
    C. know this vendor by prior dealings
    D. have dealt with this vendor before.

KEY (CORRECT ANSWERS)

1.	C	11.	B	21.	D
2.	A	12.	A	22.	C
3.	C	13.	B	23.	D
4.	B	14.	A	24.	A
5.	A	15.	B	25.	C
6.	B	16.	C	26.	B
7.	C	17.	A	27.	A
8.	B	18.	A	28.	B
9.	D	19.	B	29.	D
10.	C	20.	C	30.	D

www.ingramcontent.com/pod-product-compliance
Lightning Source LLC
Chambersburg PA
CBHW081810300426
44116CB00014B/2309